NEW ESSAYS ON ADVENTURES OF HUCKLEBERRY FINN

★ The American Novel ★

GENERAL EDITOR
Emory Elliott, Princeton University

Other books in the series:
New Essays on The Scarlet Letter
New Essays on The Great Gatsby

Forthcoming:
New Essays on Chopin's The Awakening (ed. Wendy Martin)
New Essays on The Red Badge of Courage (ed. Lee Mitchell)
New Essays on Ellison's Invisible Man (ed. Robert O'Meally)
New Essays on Light in August (ed. Michael Millgate)
New Essays on The Sun Also Rises (ed. Linda Wagner)
New Essays on James's The American (ed. Martha Banta)
New Essays on Moby-Dick (ed. Richard Brodhead)
New Essays on Uncle Tom's Cabin (ed. Eric Sundquist)

New Essays on Adventures of Huckleberry Finn

Edited by
Louis J. Budd

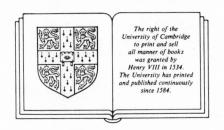

The right of the
University of Cambridge
to print and sell
all manner of books
was granted by
Henry VIII in 1534.
The University has printed
and published continuously
since 1584.

CAMBRIDGE UNIVERSITY PRESS

Cambridge

New York   New Rochelle

Melbourne   Sydney

Published by the Press Syndicate of the University of Cambridge
The Pitt Building, Trumpington Street, Cambridge CB2 1RP
32 East 57th Street, New York, NY 10022, USA
10 Stamford Road, Oakleigh, Melbourne 3166, Australia

First published 1985
Reprinted 1986, 1987, 1988

Printed in the United States of America

Library of Congress Cataloging in Publication Data
Main entry under title:
New essays on Adventures of Huckleberry Finn.
(The American novel)
Bibliography: p.
1. Twain, Mark, 1835–1910. Adventures of Huckleberry
Finn – Addresses, essays, lectures. I. Budd, Louis J.
II. Series.
PS1305.N48 1985 813'.4 85–7815
ISBN 0 521 26729 3 hard covers
ISBN 0 521 31836 X paperback

Contents

v

Contents

Series Editor's Preface

In literary criticism the last twenty-five years have been particularly fruitful. Since the rise of the New Criticism in the 1950s, which focused attention of critics and readers upon the text itself—apart from history, biography, and society—there has emerged a wide variety of critical methods which have brought to literary works a rich diversity of perspectives: social, historical, political, psychological, economic, ideological, and philosophical. While attention to the text itself, as taught by the New Critics, remains at the core of contemporary interpretation, the widely shared assumption that works of art generate many different kinds of interpretation has opened up possibilities for new readings and new meanings.

Before this critical revolution, many American novels had come to be taken for granted by earlier generations of readers as having an established set of recognized interpretations. There was a sense among many students that the canon was established and that the larger thematic and interpretative issues had been decided. The task of the new reader was to examine the ways in which elements such as structure, style, and imagery contributed to each novel's acknowledged purpose. But recent criticism has brought these old assumptions into question and has thereby generated a wide variety of original, and often quite surprising, interpretations of the classics, as well as of rediscovered novels such as Kate Chopin's *The Awakening*, which has only recently entered the canon of works that scholars and critics study and that teachers assign their students.

The aim of The American Novel Series is to provide students of American literature and culture with introductory critical guides to

American novels now widely read and studied. Each volume is devoted to a single novel and begins with an introduction by the volume editor, a distinguished authority on the text. The introduction presents details of the novel's composition, publication history, and contemporary reception, as well as a survey of the major critical trends and readings from first publication to the present. This overview is followed by four or five original essays, specifically commissioned from senior scholars of established reputation and from outstanding younger critics. Each essay presents a distinct point of view, and together they constitute a forum of interpretative methods and of the best contemporary ideas on each text.

It is our hope that these volumes will convey the vitality of current critical work in American literature, generate new insights and excitement for students of the American novel, and inspire new respect for and new perspectives upon these major literary texts.

Emory Elliott
Princeton University

1

Introduction

LOUIS J. BUDD

1

TWENTY-FIVE years after Mark Twain's death (and so, on the centennial of his birth), Mark Van Doren judged that "for better or worse he has become the author he never quite dared to hope he would have to be." The "for better or worse" indicates that by 1935 Twain was demonstrating such solid prestige that leaders of high literary culture felt timid on his behalf. They admired some feature of his artistry or of his varied writings, but they had qualms about how their approval might influence the readers for whom they felt responsible. Still, they could not decide to ignore him, primarily because *Adventures of Huckleberry Finn* had managed to establish itself as a novel that anybody with a pretence to full literacy ought to know.

More so today, people who pay any mind to books get used to hearing *Huckleberry Finn* called the great American novel, a masterpiece, a classic, and even a world classic. In this case, the terms have become interchangeable; Huck's army of admirers would think it high-falutin' to quibble about the differences. Furthermore, although many Great Books run into sullen resistance or snickers, the laurels for *Huckleberry Finn* strike readers as obviously deserved. Neither surprised nor intimidated by its rating among the tastemakers, they are amused to learn that it did not blast into a secure orbit as soon as it was published in 1884–5.

Until the 1930s, the staff of the Buffalo (New York) Public Library failed to realize that the handwritten pages for three-fifths of *Huckleberry Finn* were both sacred and valuable.[1] In 1885 its director found them in the mail "with some disappointment" because the manuscript of *Life on the Mississippi* (1883) had been hoped for instead. But not because the reviews of *Huckleberry Finn* had called it a failure. Collectively, they gave it a positive verdict, although it had not set off the ecstatic response that Mark Twain always hoped for as author, lecturer, public speaker, or promoter. The warmest reviewers proclaimed only that it had topped his previous fiction and, in particular, had achieved both deeper charm and realism than even *The Adventures of Tom Sawyer* (1876). The one prestigious critic who ranked Huck as an "immortal hero" did so almost incidentally.

Nevertheless, the direct superlatives started to come soon. In 1891, Andrew Lang, a British critic and author impressive to the clientele of the quality magazines, ranked Twain "among the greatest of contemporary makers of fiction," no doubt startling Twain's genteelist betters who ached to meet European standards. Clearly without condescension, Lang rounded off by calling *Huckleberry Finn* "the great American novel," which literary patriots had started watching for a half century ago. They, of course, recognized that Lang had written "the," not merely "a." Educated by the career of Poe's and Whitman's reputations, they could accept having native distinctiveness, along with distinction, legitimated first by a foreigner. During the 1890s, fortunately, they still much preferred a British to a French certificate of quality.

No Americans who disagreed explicitly with Lang have won enough fame themselves to catch the ear of posterity. Surely there were frowns among the Protestant ministers dabbling in literary criticism as another way of elevating a hurly-burly populace and among the professors (some of them ministers too) trying to set up departments of English as forts of scholarship. But, aside from the merits of *Huckleberry Finn*, personal history was working in Twain's favor. His bankruptcy in 1894 and then his lecture tour around the world to pay the creditors started a wave of good will that kept swelling until his death in 1910. His strictly aesthetic prestige was raised in 1896 by the announced edition of his books, which in effect declared him worthy of the same treatment as the standard authors. Of course, *Huckleberry Finn* was included in the project, which collapsed under contractual details, and in the collected editions that got going by 1899.

During the later 1890s, Twain reached the status of not only an honorific author but also, by acclamation, a popular hero and indeed the epitome of the New World, the avatar of its virtues as it in all smugness saw them. During those same years, at Harvard University, Barrett Wendell was finishing his *Literary History of America* (1900). However partial to the New England canon, he was encouraged enough by Twain's late prestige to grant that the "native use of dialects" had "resulted in at least one masterpiece, that amazing Odyssey of the Mississippi to which Mark Twain gave the fantastic name of 'Huckleberry Finn'" (p. 477). If Wendell meant the allusion to Homer more as a covert defense of his own standards than as an educated compliment, we should recognize that we have had longer to grow familiar with, even to love, the homely name of Twain's narrator. Wendell could not. In coming back to "a book which in certain moods one is disposed for all its eccentricity to call the most admirable work of literary art as yet produced on this continent," he described it as that "Odyssean story" with the "grotesque name of 'Huckleberry Finn'" (p. 503).

In 1900 Twain's homecoming after almost ten years abroad released a flood of affection and national pride, with *Huckleberry Finn* as a natural spillway. It likewise shared and also got part of the credit when Oxford University made him a Doctor of Letters, a title that was practically a license for signing masterpieces. At his death academics helped to swell the eulogies, which swept on through the postmortem essays and then books about him. He had talked so vividly and disarmingly about his faults of character that the debunkers could not find weapons, whereas the emphatic warriors for the consensus kept building his reputation, using *Huckleberry Finn* as both effect and cause. That glorious naysayer H. L. Mencken could match anybody in sounding positive too. In 1913 he presented *Huckleberry Finn* as "one of the great masterpieces of the world"; by 1919 it had improved into a "truly stupendous piece of work – perhaps the greatest novel ever written in English" – which "vastly transcends the merit of all ordinary books," "lifts itself above all hollow standard and criteria," and yet "seems greater every time I read it." Since Mencken had a gift for particularity as well as emphasis, his followers realized that they had a right to revere some parts of the novel they may have

3

merely enjoyed. In other words, *Huckleberry Finn* was already so-lidifying that basic advantage that a classic has: Readers expect it to impress them, and the cultural joggers blame themselves if it doesn't.

The disillusion after World War I incited the revolt of the young intellectuals. But, barely remembered now, a phalanx of elderly critics dominated the sober monthly magazines, and they had learned to agree that *Huckleberry Finn* is a classic. Brander Mat-thews, who had given it the warmest review of consequence in 1885, was still lecturing at Columbia University and, always a shade more enthusiastically, still writing about Twain. Since the degree from Oxford, William Lyon Phelps, famous well beyond the campus of Yale University, had played variations on the theme of Twain's genius. In 1924 he reached his highest note: "Mark Twain himself answered the query which had become almost pet-ulant by repetition, 'Who will write the great American novel?' For *Huckleberry Finn* is not only the great American novel. It is America." Such swoops of rhetoric had grown commonplace.[2] In *The Cambridge History of American Literature* (1921), Stuart P. Sher-man, speaking more deliberately for posterity, declared that *Huckleberry Finn* was "imperishably substantial." By then Huck would have felt unworthy to read his own book, which Sherman also described as Twain's "second masterpiece of Mississippi fiction."

Among the rebelling intellectuals, Van Wyck Brooks strength-ened his leadership with *The Ordeal of Mark Twain* (1920), some-times quoted yet as an irrefutable indictment. However, Brooks himself spared *Huckleberry Finn:* Twain's "whole unconscious life, the pent-up river of his own soul, had burst its bonds and rushed forth, a joyous torrent! Do we need any other explanation of the abandon, the beauty, the eternal freshness of *Huckleberry Finn?* . . . Certainly if it flies like a gay, bright, shining arrow through the tepid atmosphere of American literature, it is because of the straining of the bow, the tautness of the string, that gave it its momentum." Many authors would sell out the rest of their works for such a testimonial. Although Brooks can be suspected of overdoing praise for the exception just to make his indictment all the more striking, his readers could end up better persuaded than even by Matthews or Phelps (although not Mencken) that *Huckleberry Finn* promised a feast.

If nothing else, Brooks did it the service of stirring up Bernard DeVoto, whose passionate *Mark Twain's America* (1932) made it the apex of vernacular eloquence and free-flowing, grass-roots democracy. By reinvoking the glories of the frontier, DeVoto narrowed the shadow of the Great Depression and gratified the sudden hunger for Americana. Then after World War II he suited the consensus that the American century had dawned. Because global dominance demanded a lusty yet indigenous tradition at home, *Huckleberry Finn* fit perfectly into the undergraduate and graduate courses that began to jostle the British classics. Today most Americans meet *Huckleberry Finn* by having it "assigned" rather than stumbling on it or, if upwardly mobile in self-culture, by hunting up a copy after hearing one more superlative about it.

For college teachers, the crowning words came from two essays introducing a reprinted text. Lionel Trilling was far along toward highbrow oracularity when he boosted a paperback *Huckleberry Finn* in 1948 with extravagant praise. In 1950 T. S. Eliot, rather suddenly if belatedly parent of a classic too, went a notch further: "So we come to see Huck himself in the end as one of the permanent symbolic figures of fiction; not unworthy to take place with Ulysses, Faust, Don Quixote, Don Juan, Hamlet and other great discoveries that man has made about himself." After such praise, what dissent could matter? A reputable critic caused mostly surprise with "Why *Huckleberry Finn* Is Not the Great American Novel." His mild attack was paired with the rejoinder "Why *Huckleberry Finn* Is a Great World Novel," which expanded the field of comparison back to at least Eliot's sweep.[3] When the novel paraded through its centennial year, its stature was seldom challenged on campus – or off, so far as serious discussion of fiction carries on beyond a curriculum.

Many kinds of facts now support the towering rhetoric, the almost ferocious superlatives; and the sales or reprintings grow into impressive patterns.[4] Deluxe editions compete, and no set of Great Books dares to leave out *Huckleberry Finn*. Although such sets usually end up as furniture, the paperback editions protect it from Twain's jeer about the classic as "a book which people praise and don't read." Critics in many languages and sales in about every language that is printed have widened the fame of *Huckleberry Finn*, encouraging a still warmer pride of ownership among Americans. Even literary academics, no longer defensive about provinciality, like to agree that it distills the homiest truths about the United States, yet achieves a universal weight of reference. At the same time, Huck as a semidetached character weaves through commercial ads, cartoons, casual quotations, and greeting cards, returning to the folk culture he started from.

But Twain's fellow artists, domestic or foreign, have accepted *Huckleberry Finn* as a new standard of originality. Because of a terseness that reinforces the sweep, Ernest Hemingway's tribute that "all modern American literature comes from" it is quoted more often than any other. The many imitators of Huck's voice and attitudes usually give humble credit through allusions, and a few have decided on full disclosure. John Seelye, wanting to liberate Twain posthumously from genteel censorship, has wittily imagined *The True Adventures of Huckleberry Finn* (1970). Greg Matthews, a young Australian who dwarfs the explicators of Huck's closing paragraph, fills five hundred pages with *The Further Adventures of Huckleberry Finn* (1983). Surely neither novelist dreamed, more wildly than Tom Sawyer, of such glory as outdoing the real thing.

As classics go, *Huckleberry Finn*, although outlasting many a rival trumpeted by reviewers, is quite young. That raises a point of semantics. For centuries, down through the early part of our own, classics, whether or not in Sanscrit or Greek or Latin originally, were by definition very old. They transmitted high culture of the past, or, more demonstrably, certified that their devotee had acquired it in the present. With utmost learning and subtlety, Frank Kermode distinguishes two species: the works that, we think, encapsulated an era and thus allow us to reenter it mentally and the works that have stated our basic humanity so well as to triumph over time and space. *Huckleberry Finn* has moved its admirers to make either of these claims for it, or both. However, Kermode goes on to argue that any texts we hand along as classics "possess also an openness to accommodation which keeps them alive under endlessly varying dispositions," that they escape from the bulldozer of novelty by mediating the tension between "the enduring and the transient."[5] This principle applies better to *Huckleberry Finn* than most of the works he names. They are too seldom discussed to have proved their innate adaptability, but *Huckleberry Finn* has survived under dizzying changes in interpretation. Although Kermode would take this as exemplifying his point that classics are "naive" texts, unusually open to re-vision, another possibility is that critics enjoy *Huckleberry Finn* so fundamentally that they feel driven to fit it into their frame of assumptions by simply ignoring some passages.

The longer one thinks, the harder it gets to bracket *Huckleberry Finn* with the *Odyssey, Aeneid, Divine Comedy,* or *Paradise Lost.* Although Trilling's and Eliot's seal may have validated it for elitists, it naggingly seems less starchy and ambitious than the textbook monuments, including *Don Quixote.* Trilling and Eliot increased their credibility by invoking myth, essentially religious at that, to which their Jungian cohorts have added a version of depth psychology. Yet a reader who respects the kind of novel that developed during the eighteenth century cannot help feeling that *Huckleberry Finn* belongs to a range of mountains in mass popularity – *Charlotte Temple,* several of Dicken's books, *Jane Eyre, Uncle Tom's Cabin,* and *Little Women,* for example. Andrew Lang was the first critic to express that feeling, although he quarreled with modish snobbery rather than the classical tradition when he derided "culture's modern disciples" as a "mere crowd of very slimly educated people, who have no natural taste or impulse." In fact, a few formalists still shrug off *Huckleberry Finn* as a crude try at Henry James's idea of a novel.

Mencken and DeVoto raged at such sneers, with obvious gratitude for the chance to do so. Nobody has presumed to carry on their tone, but some later enthusiasts have proposed that *Huckleberry Finn* is not only about, but at its best belongs to, the folk mind. One imaginative essay associates Twain and Charlie Chaplin as "popular mythmakers."[6] It interprets them as appealing primarily to folk wisdom and, without contradiction, to the old taste for theatricality, for melodramatic strokes. When these appeals work, the faults of structure that might offend a connoisseur of cerebral patterns will raise no hackles. The approach from popular culture can even argue that the "formal flaws" in *Huckleberry Finn* may please mass taste, "for all we know." More satisfyingly, since many naive readers consciously want to elevate their taste, Twain, instead of being tolerated as the "highbrow's lowbrow," can be welcomed functionally as the "lowbrow's highbrow."

Huckleberry Finn will survive any such tug-of-war. Its sophisticated admirers will keep on etherealizing it in their quarterlies and will assign it to students, including non–English majors. Its mass-cult consumers will keep on proving their loyalty not only by paying for copies or borrowing from a public library but also by piling up profits for the hucksters who exploit any popular image. It has become firmly institutionalized through a process described best by Barbara Herrnstein Smith: "Repeatedly cited and recited, translated, taught and imitated, and thoroughly enmeshed in the network of intertextuality that continuously *constitutes* the high culture of the orthodoxly educated population," *Huckleberry Finn* can, like other classics, "perform a large number of various functions" for intellectuals.[7] Yet its characters will contribute to new "theme" parks across the United States and will always draw families of tourists to Hannibal.

The uses for *Huckleberry Finn* lay a practical responsibility on critics and teachers: They must insist on a professionally edited, authentic text. Careless reprints, although a problem, do far less harm than the jaggedly shortened, bowdlerized, or even rearranged editions marketed for secondary schools.[8] Unappeased, a few humorless parents have included *Huckleberry Finn* in their campaign to censor textbooks and library shelves. Since its sexuality can offend only the most prudish vigilantes, the prettified versions often distort instead its social or ethical thrust so badly that outright banning would be better. Fortunately, several good editions are available, although none equals the standard of the Iowa/California text, which also reproduces the illustrations that Twain carefully supervised.

2

Twain's personality had many, sometimes clashing, sides that make *Huckleberry Finn* especially hard to fit into the shape of his career. There are more than enough biographical facts to jar dog-matism or feed combativeness. There are so many suggestive clues that, for the critical enterprise anyway, it becomes best to focus on two perspectives: on what generations of scholars have called "in-fluences" on a work of art; and, far more challenging nowadays, on Twain's "intentions" in and for *Huckleberry Finn*.

Anybody curious about whether real-life persons or events are buried in *Huckleberry Finn* learns that prospectors started digging early. Albert Bigelow Paine, Twain's official, live-in biographer, favored this kind of material so eagerly that he welcomed legend whenever the facts were thin, murky, or simply inferior. In *Mr. Clemens and Mark Twain* (1966), Justin Kaplan, although improv-ing on Paine in many ways, favored details and guesses that point-ed to the psychic sources of the major books. More minutely and cautiously, Walter Blair's *Mark Twain & Huck Finn* (1960) explored every visible approach through Twain's experiences, friendships, literary models, and general reading. Although seldom proved wrong, Blair has been supplemented by small finds and huge guesses, whereas hopes for a major strike encourage further dig-ging. As Alan Gribben's facts and mini-essays in *Mark Twain's Library: A Reconstruction* (1977) are absorbed, new trails of influ-ence will be laid out, maybe even accepted. But the sources for *Huckleberry Finn* already established are so clear that every sound critic uses them not only in the polished explication but also in the process of rejecting tentative hypotheses.

From a commercial perspective, Twain's intention was simple even if *Huckleberry Finn* ended up with competing centennials – of its first British printing in 1884 and its American one in 1885. He meant for it to sell boomingly. More specifically, he meant it to charm the public who now and then bought a book by subscrip-tion, that is, gave in to a salesman (actually, often a woman) who went from door to door. Because it was published by the firm Twain had lately set up, he controlled the marketing along with the editing – an author's daydream. Surely his double stake in the sales restrained him from the extreme violations of taboos that a few critics discover in *Huckleberry Finn* today. Although early re-views show that it did offend the morally overanxious, he had toned down the rawness of the native humorists whose traits are double-helixed in it.[9] He did not, however, allow himself the luxury of intending it as a work of "literature" in the nineteenth-century sense.

Twain's royalities let him feel that at least his books provided well for his wife and three daughters. As a family man, he merged into the good citizen who was accumulating a respect too pleasant to sacrifice for a burst of blatant self-indulgence. The record of his sociopolitical engagement is plain, highlighted by his part in the presidential elections of 1876, 1880, and 1884. Of course, he could have been fulfilling, more than usual, several of his personalities, could have been, as a novelist, escaping on a raft from his family and its expensive demands. Or, to project his intention from the crassest motives, he could have decided that business is business, no matter how strongly he abhorred southern racism; undeniably, Jim's run to freedom gets sidetracked when the entertaining King and the Duke wander into the plot. Or, to speculate about attitudes rather than deliberate motives, Twain was doing mightily well as a capitalist. Why should he rebel against the basic system, against the historical and economic march of progress if it had not yet achieved full justice? Because Jim emerges so appealingly through his comradeship with Huck, we can overrate its relevance, planned or effectual, for the situation of the freed slaves in the 1880s. Finally, although Twain had a keen social conscience and although politics ran through his writings from the Hannibal years on, his instinct for comic play also poured into *Huckleberry Finn*.

Allowing him too little self-control, critics oriented by depth psychology have traced grooves of unintended intention. With proof from biography when they can induce it, some uncover Freudian patterns.[10] Many a less clinical critic has argued that Twain unknowingly confessed to dark, even death-loving impulses by surrounding Huck with violence. It is reasonable to agree that Twain felt crueler psychic pressures than most of us. Otherwise, he would not have evolved into the instinctive humorist who could create a *Huckleberry Finn*.

But often the private Twain had to adjust to the needs of the public figure. Deciding that by 1880–1 Twain "was well on his way to achieving the eminence of a national institution," Justin Kaplan judges too harshly that the "obligations of such celebrity, which at times he accepted with delight, were self-imitation, constant exposure, and performance." Still, by putting "Mark Twain" on the title page of *Huckleberry Finn,* the author was keenly aware of using not just a pen name but the billing of a showman particularly successful as a lecturer. Twain made his newest book and the barnstorming tour with George Washington Cable in 1884–5 publicize each other. A biographer has to speculate on whether he intended *Huckleberry Finn* to fuse his showman and his literary images better or to push the emphasis to one side. He was, we now remember only condescendingly, starting his hardest run as an entrepreneur. In a simpler form of the problem, any capable biographer must sketch the target audience for *Huckleberry Finn.* Twain insisted that they could not have it until 40,000 orders were racked up. When the Concord (Massachusetts) Public Library, to the applause of editorialists here and there, rejected it as coarse, he doubtless felt insulted, but he gloated that the publicity would help sales. He calculated that his grass-roots strength counted more, in any sense, than the frowns of Concord, itself a target lately for breezy humorists.

This strength partly depended, he realized, on his previous books. It is challenging to speculate whether he thought he was making a major break with them, and if so, whether he was raising or lowering his aesthetic sights. Did he think he had taken a noble risk that might hurt the backlist sales of *The Prince and the Pauper* and *Life on the Mississippi*? Or, less heroically, did confidence in his roaring celebrity assure him that he could suit himself with a vernacular spokesman? On the other hand, gratitude for the result of that decision should not stop us from wondering if a hunger for popularity limited as much as it encouraged his commitment to that spokesman; Twain ridiculed Huck and led him into self-ridicule more than the logic of the plot demands. If we get beyond our delight in Twain–Huck as a poet of the vernacular, we start suspecting other ambivalences. Why couldn't Twain carry that poetry over into "Tom and Huck Among the Indians" or, after ten years of refilling his psychic tank, into *Tom Sawyer Abroad* and *Tom Sawyer, Detective*? If the vernacular had liberated his deepest emotions for the first time, how could he insist on presenting *Huckleberry Finn* as a sequel to *The Adventures of Tom Sawyer*? Generally bound in green, it was also advertised with a blue cover to match the earlier novel.

A biographical approach to the manuscript itself raises challenging questions about the course of its composition. Did it germinate as a loving sequel to *Tom Sawyer* or, more than the change of narrator signals, as a rejection of boyish nostalgia? Do we comprehend yet why the handwritten pages piled up in sporadic batches? The gaps left in *The Tragedy of Pudd'nhead Wilson* force us to doubt that Twain, notoriously impatient, would dovetail the parts of *Huckleberry Finn* composed during a jumbled, eventful period of seven years.[11] Could even a better-disciplined writer manage to mortise and tenon the two main sections of manuscript from 1876 to 1883? The now familiar question of unity or overall symmetry will reappear in the four essays that follow this introduction.

3

For readers charmed by Huck's language, the period when the novel was written or even its stated time of action does not seem all that long ago. They slip back into a vanished river culture with warmer empathy than they can work up for the society of Lewis's *Main Street* or Dos Passos's *U.S.A.* Like *The Scarlet Letter* and *Moby-Dick*, the usual peers of *Huckleberry Finn* for those who nominate American masterpieces of the nineteenth century by threes, it has an exotic flavor. Yet it feels close to ordinary experience. Asserting the universality of a great classic for *Huckleberry Finn* does not explain enough. It not only rose out of a firm historical context, but it stands forth more sharply when seen against Twain's time and place and, in turn, makes them blindingly familiar.

Anybody who has tried to hone a sense of American history can migrate into Huck's world with special ease because of both the "frontier thesis" and the career of racism. Heightened for Twainians by DeVoto, the vision of the West as a haven of democracy, individualism, and pioneer ingenuity lives on. For a few romantics, escape to somewhere, as they take Huck to be proposing, is still possible. Likewise, the color-ridden, Faulknerian South and therefore the antebellum culture it descends from stick in our

12

imagination. Actually, by 1885 the dominant North was already dominated by urbanism, technology, bureaucracy in industry as well as government, and machine politics. Twain protected himself from rigorous historians by giving the time of action vaguely as "forty to fifty years" earlier and avoiding unshakable clues like the name of a sitting president. Nevertheless, strangely but impressively, many later readers have assumed that *Huckleberry Finn* speaks to and about the society they are struggling through.

Those who claim historical accuracy or impact for it both help and hurt its reputation misleadingly. It can get far too much credit for relevance in 1885 to an age of Wall Street barons, the rise of industrial and then banking monopolies, the recruiting for imperialism, and Populist militance in that same Mississippi Valley. Was there any territory left that Huck could escape to for long, ahead of the settlers and boomers?[12] To the extent that Twain himself doubted that possibility, we have to smile at Huck's plan as uninformed. Likewise, we need to decide how distinctly Twain wanted to draw a parallel with the situation of the emancipated slaves twenty years after the Civil War. The power brokers, having struck a deal after the election of 1876, were pushing the blacks toward their nadir in the first decade of the twentieth century. Does Jim essentially challenge the paternalism that Uncle Remus is happy to accept from Joel Chandler Harris, who admired the novel heartily? Some of Jim's descendants have started to attack its reputation for scorning racism, accepted even by Marxist critics, and in 1983 a black publisher, previously an administrator for a high school, edited out the word "nigger." Deservedly more influential, Ralph Ellison objects that "Jim's friendship for Huck comes across as that of a boy for another boy rather than as the friendship of an adult for a junior."[13]

An old critical question is whether it is possible to appreciate a novel properly without reentering the author's day-to-day context, which may be more compelling than the times written about when they are still more distant. An avid consumer of newspapers, Twain continually expressed topical attitudes. In his mind, the Grangerford–Shepherdson feud, to us apparently a purely antebellum touch, satirized a contemporary problem. Less insistently, his vignette of the "softy, soothering undertaker" projected a belief that ground burial had become archaic and unsanitary. Although the Tom Sawyer made foolish by romantic books stretched back to Don Quixote, he also served a then contemporary breed of double agents, of enemies within the gates. Many novelists were appeasing their middle-class audience with characters whose common sense – and, if women, their virginal caution – was muddled by reading fiction.

Inevitably, time develops another bothersome effect. If, like the reader-response critics, we hold that a novel exists only as it is being experienced by someone who thus becomes the author's collaborator, then its frame of reference shifts toward the moment whenever that process is occurring. A radical of the 1980s interacts with *Huckleberry Finn* differently even from such a prescient liberal as Randolph Bourne, who, well ahead of the intellectuals' contempt for the 1920s, perceived Twain as "reassuring every American in his self-complacency." On the other hand, Wilsonian idealism, so long as it lasted into that decade, could encourage Americans to admire Huck as both innocent and redemptive. The Great Depression, unexpectedly, taught some readers to romanticize Huck's kind of folks; as a publisher's blurb might say, if you liked Sandburg's *The People, Yes* (1936) and Steinbeck's *The Grapes of Wrath* (1939), you'd love *Huckleberry Finn*.

The context of literature also includes the history of the canon, that slowly changing roll of works that reach the summit of their genre and deserve any mission that the establishment can find for them.[14] Inescapably, the claims then validating the canon affected the early reactions to *Huckleberry Finn*. During the 1880s, the canon itself was reaching its high point of authority under Matthew Arnold's stern ideal of the best that had been thought and said by humankind. Many attacks on *Huckleberry Finn* applied a somewhat new principle; instead of belaboring novels in general, as they would have done a hundred or fifty years before, they scolded it as unworthy of its kind. When critics increasingly accepted it as worthy, they found reasons for proving that it satisfied the rules for a novel of lasting value after all. When they refined those rules into a sophisticated genre, they invoked symmetries of form to cover and even justify the political retreat that underlay Tom's toying with Jim in the Evasion sequence.

Meanwhile, DeVoto, a delighted enemy of formalisms, was insisting not on the abstract fitness but on the lyricism, energy, freshness, and liberating humor of Huck's language. More systematically, Walter Blair was following up the same idea, which encouraged Henry Nash Smith to develop his impressive, influential case for the healthy subversiveness of the vernacular.[15] Today it is standard academic wisdom that Twain's central, precedent-setting achievement is Huck's language. Unfortunately, Twain's marvelously flexible, resourceful, rhythmic, and spacious style, perfected over decades and adapted to a range of works, is often made synonymous with Huck's, which is too limited for Twain's resonances no matter how daringly it was stretched in a few passages. In other words, Twain gets the gold medal for having defied and thus reconstituted the canon, but its adjusted criteria undervalue his other writings when they sound too little like *Huckleberry Finn*. Those criteria also ignore the fact that many readers approach it with warm expectations based on his broader career, especially as a lecturer and compelling personality.[16]

4

Once *Huckleberry Finn* is accepted as literature, it is evaluated, if only implicitly, by comparison with respected novels and within a framework of aesthetic theory. Before taking individual critics on their terms, we should especially prepare to avoid two mistakes. First, we need to cope with the fact that the clamor of opinions can get numbing; any imaginative work that is worth discussing causes tumultuous disagreement. *Huckleberry Finn* is a living text, perhaps not even fully aged in this sense, much less sloping toward oblivion. Every likely critic feels compelled to give it a whirl sooner or later. In weary moments, having skimmed one more explication that is stale or just plain silly, we groan about a Tower of Babble. However, if steadied by a perspective on the long-range process, we can learn selectively from the uproar and even hope for future wisdom from it. The second easy mistake would be to judge the critics along a historical sequence while expecting that our age will have announced the right dogma. The school for modernism never graduates its final class or lacks for junior faculty.

The past twenty years have seethed with new systems of criticism. This intensity has often included scorn for any difference of opinion. But I hope it is still possible to profile the critics of *Huckleberry Finn* fairly. Because it has great charms it must, presumably, come close to perfection. Any approach, however, that dulls the shimmering particularity of *Huckleberry Finn* is suspect. We should worry less about "incorrect responses than insufficient ones."[17]

5

The notion that *Huckleberry Finn* was at first ignored by the cultural establishment suits our contempt toward the genteelists (like Miss Watson, "a tolerable slim old maid with goggles on") who oppressed children with their standards in decorum. Some good scholars have prolonged that notion because they searched the solid monthly magazines instead of the newspapers, which paid more attention to subscription publishing. Respect for the New England canon has emphasized the reaction by the overseers of the Concord Free Public Library. Without aiming to justify their censorship, a critic grounded in popular literature widens the gap among publics by speculating that "common readers" enjoyed *Huckleberry Finn* as "lowbrow 'escape' fiction," as a "pleasing and familiar package" of a "western locale, the picturesque adventures of its raffish characters, and the strongly subversive stance of its vagabond hero"[18] The dime-novel tradition still demands an answer from anyone who contemplates Huck only under the cold light of eternity.

By 1885, Twain had built an audience cutting into all levels of literacy. Thirty years later, spinning yarns for his autobiography, he recalled that the banning in Concord brought a "number of letters of sympathy and indignation," although – improbably – they were "mainly from children, I am obliged to admit." Actually, the only two reviews in the magazines were highly favorable: by Brander Matthews in a grave British weekly and by a respected New Englander in the *Century*, lately risen to leadership among the monthlies that honored middle-class earnestness.[19] The *Century* also printed about a fourth of *Huckleberry Finn*, which got humbler yet broader exposure through long excerpts in several big-city dailies and through Twain's program for his barnstorming tour with George Washington Cable during the winter of 1884–5. As a group, these excerpts featured the King and the Duke, stirring events, and the seriocomic debates between Huck and Jim. In effect, they brought on another, unwritten set of reviews, clearly favorable from the live audiences anyway. The mere fact that three issues of the *Century* had printed selections aroused mostly approving comment.

We now can talk more accurately about the written reviews because first-class research shows that over a dozen newspapers chimed in, their reactions ranging from outraged propriety to rapture.[20] Then the banning in Concord set off a much louder round of reviews, editorials, and second thoughts. *Huckleberry Finn* did not lose this round, nor did every New England newspaper praise the Concordians, who, on the other hand, got support beyond the Alleghenies too. But it did not win a clear-cut decision either. The main issue had become its worthiness as moral doctrine, particularly for the young, and some of its supporters turned apologetic, intimidated by the self-deluding idealism that would enrage Ernest Hemingway's cohort into despising the genteel tradition. However, enough adults voted yes with their dollars so that *Huckleberry Finn* rolled on, soon matching *The Adventures of Tom Sawyer* in steady sales.

Especially at the start, *Tom Sawyer* (1876) has clearly influenced the critical context of *Huckleberry Finn*. The echo in the titles, the subtitle of the later novel (*Tom Sawyer's Comrade*), and its opening words ("You don't know about me, without you have read a book by the name of *Tom Sawyer*") raise certain expectations. They also invite friendly comparisons, and for decades the critics followed the obvious course. Not until the 1950s, in spite of Hemingway's earlier advice to ignore the last eleven chapters of *Huckleberry Finn*, did Tom emerge as a liability. Twain had made him the central figure in Huck's further narratives (although Greg Matthews quickly leaves him behind), and obituary cartoons in 1910 showed the boys as inseparable, even for rafting. The pairing has continued in many joint editions of the *Adventures* and in pop art while decreasing among critics ever since *Huckleberry Finn* was elevated to a class by itself.[21] Young readers often come to *Tom*

Sawyer first and carry over a mind set that may make the later novel disappointing. Several scenes – painting the fence, Tom watching his own funeral service, and the gropings in the cave – remain more vivid for them than any that Huck describes. Because his vernacular, like Robert Frost's talksong, resists translation, *Tom Sawyer* competes vigorously abroad and colors grownup reactions to what not many aesthetically sophisticated Americans now care to consider its sequel.

Whatever the linkages with *Tom Sawyer*, the prestige of *Huckleberry Finn* took an almost puzzling jump during its first decade. It was soon helped by the quality of the public tributes that poured in for Twain's fiftieth birthday in November 1885. That was the turning point in his march toward heroic stature, surprisingly benefitted in 1894 by sympathy over his bankruptcy, which in turn brought on his celebrated lecture tour around the world to honor his debts. Meanwhile, a growing self-confidence in American taste allowed respect for a vernacular hero, especially one wreathed in nostalgia for the preindustrial village. To be sure, that confidence was still shaky enough to prize outside agreement, such as when *Punch* praised *Huckleberry Finn* as "Homeric . . . in the true sense, as no other English book is." Most fundamentally, abroad and at home, the pleasure in its quality must have been spreading by word of mouth. A reprinting by Harper's became "the occasion of almost universal approbation" in 1896.[22] The New York *Critic* remarked that "it would probably be difficult to find many cultured people who have not read the story, but it would be even more difficult . . . to find many cultured people who do not desire to read it again." Twain doubtless liked the compliment from this weekly for the bookish; but demotic strength meant far bigger sales, and he may have preferred the mild intimidation in a Philadelphia newspaper: "We are suspicious of the middle-aged person who has not read *Huckleberry Finn*."

Even so, it probably benefited more than it helped, since the admiration for Twain as a personality kept swelling, encouraged at home by such triumphs as his popularity in Vienna, glamorous capital of the Austro-Hungarian Empire. Americans particularly noticed every fresh bouquet from England, such as "My Favorite Novelist and His Best Book" by Sir Walter Besant, admired both as a writer and a humanitarian. Yale awarded Twain a D.Litt. degree in 1902, and soon the University of Missouri fittingly did the same. He had written serious art, it more and more appeared, and not simply humor. In 1904 he was among the first seven members in the American Academy elected by the National Institute of Arts and Letters. All along, W. D. Howells, the oracle on fiction and a novelist far more eminent than Twain, had been gilding his crony's reputation, although usually with emphasis on the reformist side.[23] His essay "Mark Twain: An Inquiry" (1901) did hedge with "I who like *A Connecticut Yankee in King Arthur's Court* so much have half a mind to give my whole heart to *Huckleberry Finn.*" Yet he habitually paired the Tom and Huck books for commentary. In 1897, Brander Matthews had added *Pudd'nhead Wilson* to discuss a trinity of Mississippi Valley novels. As various collected editions came out, reviewers seldom named *Huckleberry Finn* as unarguably, blindingly, the jewel in the crown. In fact, a few of them still tingled from the old impact of *The Innocents Abroad* (1869).

By 1910 many of the elegies had come from fellow novelists rather than humorists. However, Arnold Bennett, because both *Tom Sawyer* and *Huckleberry Finn* are "magnificent" just "episodically," started the idea, attractive enough to last for at least fifty years, that Twain was a "divine amateur." Foreshadowing the rigors of formalism (which would prove hard on his own work), he regretted that Twain "never would or never could appreciate the fact . . . that the most important thing in any work of art is its construction." But, for the time being, impressionistic criticism was in fashion. Through its flair for enthusiasm, it attracted more readers for Twain than cerebral expounding could ever claim to do. Mencken, rising toward his bumptious but riveting authority as a tastemaker, seized any chance to sing the praises of *Huckleberry Finn* while firmly holding *Tom Sawyer* to an inferior level.

Soon after Twain's death, while the general reader was absorbed in Archibald Henderson's vigorous homage (1911) and Albert Bigelow Paine's worshipping volumes (1912), critics started to shake off the charm of his personality. Furthermore, a widened range of jobs for intellectuals and the solidifying of literature as an academic field let criticism develop into a profession with self-conscious standards. Whenever those standards changed, they settled into the next consensus quickly:

> Twentieth century criticism of Mark Twain has followed the general course of American criticism. It has been influenced by the impressionism of the years before the First World War, the search for a usable part during the 1920's, the cult of realism and of social significance during the 1930's, the emphasis on technique that became fashionable in the later 1930's and 1940's, and the interest in symbolism, often involving psychological speculation, that has rather paradoxically flourished along with formalism in recent years.[24]

This survey added the warning, still useful now, that Twain "poses special problems" because "criticism is notoriously helpless in the presence of writing that is really funny." The warning was already needed in 1920 when Van Wyck Brooks's *The Ordeal of Mark Twain* announced the time of reckoning for another outdated reputation.

Past the heat of battle, we can see that Brooks was primarily attacking the faults in American character, devoted to bourgeois prosperity, that had emasculated Twain and that continued as a clear and present danger.[25] Obviously implying the compliment that Twain's genius was worth his anger, which exempted *Huckleberry Finn* anyway, he went far beyond Howells or Paine in taking Twain's career seriously, in connecting it to issues that would determine the fate of Western culture. Such portentousness eventually benefited Twain's reputation more than Brooks's later, still richer praise for *Huckleberry Finn*. However, those who consider *The Ordeal of Mark Twain* a fertility dance rather than a logical argument think that its finest result was to stir up DeVoto.

Contemptuous of any notion that *Huckleberry Finn* was a psychic truancy, DeVoto made it the centerpiece of *Mark Twain's America* (1932). Afterward, more calmly, he described his book as "what a later fashion came to call a 'social' study of literature. It was grounded, that is, in a belief that a writer's environment is important to his work and that, specifically, much of what was great and fruitful in Mark Twain's books was an expression of a national

20

experience."[26] And *Huckleberry Finn* had stated the quintessence: "Here is America" with its "life formed into fiction." This capped the eagerness, perceptible since at least 1896, to acclaim the strongly localized Huck as, paradoxically, archetypal of the vast New World. Dependent emotionally on the myth of manifest destiny, this acclaim assumed that the qualities he encapsulated were totally admirable. In a throbbing counterpoint, DeVoto, who would later write first-class histories, also presented *Huckleberry Finn* as embodying the manliest side of the westering frontier. This idea had been sounded earlier, most notably in Howells's declaring Twain "the Lincoln of our literature," but after DeVoto it was popular in rhetoric that did not intend to face cross-examination.

DeVoto's praises have become a subliminal tang of *Huckleberry Finn*. Because of his other accomplishments, he soon carried greater weight with the professoriate than Brooks, and his further writing about Twain used sources with a scrupulosity they could trust. Retracting none of his enthusiasms while exploring the brooding solemnity of *Huckleberry Finn*, "a dark book, as dark a book as Moby-Dick," his *Mark Twain at Work* (1942) made what is still the most persuasively ambitious, many-sided, and eloquent case for it overall. Meanwhile, tamer scholars were finishing books and articles that connected an elusive genius better with some of his millions of printed words. Edward Wagenknecht's *Mark Twain: The Man and His Work* (1935) assumed that it dealt with a world-class artist (although a "divine amateur" at times) and that *Huckleberry Finn* was his peak; J. DeLancey Ferguson's concisely excellent *Mark Twain: Man and Legend* (1943) argued for his professionalism and integrity of purpose. But the paradigm was changing. Academics had started to treat *Huckleberry Finn* as not just Twain's finest book but the chief reason for caring about him. For several reasons, however, this did not mean that his fame was narrowing into a repetitive litany.

Perceiving that Twain had been "taken over by the professors" during the 1930s, Henry Nash Smith decided that if this "shift in jurisdiction has proved a mixed blessing," it "has tended to inhibit the vagaries of speculation that Brooks's rather autocratic treatment of fact had encouraged."[27] Smith, it happened, was welcoming caution just as the drive for originality was starting up the freewheeling explications of the 1960s and 1970s. No flow of interest catches all the professors, however, nor does every devotee of fact have to be owlish. Convincingly yet appreciatively, Walter Blair began applying his expertise in "native" humor. Instead of rhapsodizing about the frontier, he measured Twain's uniqueness against what he had learned from his forerunners and peers. Still, *Huckleberry Finn* had expanded beyond anybody's map, whereas every new approach hurried to confront it. A mini-exhibit in the study and teaching of literature, it became the over-my-dead-body issue for faculty who opposed admitting American authors into the curriculum of English departments.

The mid-1940s began another sharp, jostling change in that curriculum, which soon favored concentration upon technique, structure, and deep meanings. Such closer reading did not bring unanimity either, and three of the four essays that stand out from the next cycle were as sweeping as ever. Although Leslie Fiedler's "Come Back to the Raft Ag'in, Huck Honey" unmasked several classics, its discovery that Huck and Jim's comradeship was latently a "Sacred Marriage of males" caused the heaviest shock, not softened much because Fiedler transferred the stimulus from Twain's id to the hangups of a racist society. But Fiedler made such leaps of logic that they were hard not only to cope with but also to support on a classroom level. Lionel Trilling and T. S. Eliot brought suavity and immense prestige among the faculty to their introductions to inexpensive reprints. Trilling encouraged awe for "one of the world's great books" whose "intense and even complex moral quality" beatifies a tiny "community of saints" devoted to a "river-god."[28] This homage included the style — "not less than definitive in American literature" — and the closing chapters for their "certain formal aptness." Eliot, evidently on his own, had been reaching a highly similar judgment. Whereas his argument that "neither a tragic nor a happy ending would be suitable" and so Huck "can only disappear" behind a "cloud of whimsicalities" sounded more apologetic, he capitalized the mythic quality into a River God. A French critic jeered that Eliot's cachet intimidated those who liked to warn that the book was overrated by adults because they had enjoyed it as children. More positively, some elitist American critics used Eliot as a chance to come in from the cold.

Leo Marx's essay, probably the most often reprinted of the four, soon attacked Trilling's and Eliot's case for the ending chapters because it showed no regret for the loss of the moral thrust that had been accumulating through Huck's inner development. This appeal to content over form was welcomed by a political trend with which Marx sympathized. During the 1950s, observes Daniel Hoffman, "critical opinion at last recognized the inherent dignity of Jim." In fact, a Marxist historian had proclaimed him the "real hero" whose "nobility shines through the entire book."[29] As the civil rights movement boomed, such respect grew common, sometimes tinged with anger for his having to hide under a stereotype; a still tougher probing eventually suggested that he has more guile than liberals want to see, that − experienced in puttin' on ole massa − Jim could manipulate Huck for his own desperate goals. Laying a different line of strength for him, Hoffman would ennoble Jim not only for "his emergence toward manhood through the exercise of his freedom" but still more for his "supernatural power as interpreter of the oracles of nature." Although no partisan of Jim has as yet praised the ending sequence, it does continue to recruit admirers who warily acknowledge Leo Marx as the lion in the path.

Aside from racial politics −whether stated or else denied yet implicit − the criticism of the 1950s brought full employment for *Huckleberry Finn*. So many essays were published that only a glib daily columnist would dare to account for all of them. There was at least some enthusiasm on every major heading. For instance, an inspection of the "moral structure" found masterful "clarity and directness of insight"; a scholar-critic known for his severity concluded, after intense analysis of technique: "The total result of these thematic, structural and symbolic workings is a novel which has a remarkably high degree of consistency, coherence, and unity."[30] The most influential essay of the later 1950s, still often quoted as gospel, was Henry Nash Smith's introduction for what also was the best-edited text. Using a literary rationale, he expounded the contrast (foreshadowed by Trilling) between Huck and Jim's fragile community out on the river and the corrupted society on the shore. The King and the Duke, of course, counted for the depravity of the shore.

Since the 1950s, inventing an approach to *Huckleberry Finn* has become a triumph in itself. It can be published for its improbable novelty, like one more way of curing a cold or of losing weight while eating heartily. At the other extreme, essays that rebottle old tonics can slip past a busy editor. The good news is that a consensus has been gathering on some points. Commonplaces of Twain criticism that Smith discussed as recent in 1963 have lasted until now. One of those commonplaces — that Twain raced daringly up and down a range of comic personae — has particularly led deeper into the text. As the complexities of Huck's character are matched with his use of language (not just vocabulary), genuine subtleties emerge more visibly, and further insights from that perspective are likely.

During the 1960s, teachers could learn from or assign six collections of reprinted essays about *Huckleberry Finn*, besides at least one book annually about its author. Most impressive of all was *Mark Twain: The Development of a Writer* (1962) by Henry Nash Smith, the winner of major prizes for *Virgin Land: The American West as Symbol and Myth* (1950). In asking how *Huckleberry Finn* is a masterpiece, he set a new level of discrimination for identifying the effects of its commitment to a vernacular spokesman. Although Smith prefers an interdisciplinary rationale, Twain would stay primarily in literature courses once they had adopted him. Specialization, with its technical vocabulary and savage contempt for amateurs, builds barbed-wire fences. As yet, the Popular Culture movement has not tried to annex Twain, maybe because it wants to avoid the mistake that American Studies made by overemphasizing the world of print.

By the early 1960s, nobody was surprised when a group was organized to give Twain the meticulous editing proposed for the classic American authors. So many problems turned up that the pace has been agonizingly slow. Furthermore, because the organizers knew that the text of *Huckleberry Finn* would draw the heaviest traffic, they went at it very cautiously. Finally available, it will stimulate many more essays, although Walter Blair and others

24

may have already followed up the major clues in the manuscripts that Twain saved for us. The flush times that founded the ambitious editions also granted a lighter teaching load to most professors, so that more of them could write about *Huckleberry Finn.* Reaching back to 1885 without apology, *Modern Fiction Studies* devoted a "symposium" of nine essays to it alone in 1968.

The 1970s – to keep using neat partitions –established a level of more responsible reading as critics, educated by the previous commentary, have been sensitized to some motif or context they might have undervalued. That commentary goes on growing enthusiastically. Many a panoramic book insists on a side trip into *Huckleberry Finn;* most biographies of the American spirit feel obliged to work it in. Its dignity as a basic document can lead to judgments that it is "certainly a very sad book." Such portentousness or an always flashier fringe of ingenuity is mercifully balanced by what Geoffrey Hartman belittles as Common Sense criticism. For example, Edwin H. Cady begins: "In the light of common day, which was characteristically Clemens's light, his masterpiece appears more realistic than a reading of the bulk of critical discussion during the past two decades would give one warrant to believe." Cady goes on to distinguish between its "negative" realism as antiromantic burlesque and the stunningly authentic mimesis of other episodes; also, he brilliantly resets it within a subgenre of the "boy's book" that had burgeoned during the 1870s. Another critic grounded in the realistic tradition protests that we are too eager to make Huck an "angel in homespun."[31] More important, he demonstrates that the three main interpretations of the moral absolutes latent in the plot persist in talking past each other.

The still rising eminence of *Huckleberry Finn* was exemplified by two essays lengthy enough to be issued as books.[32] One – moving with the then latest ventures in theory – identifies Twain's structuralist principle as the ability he gave his characters to seize control of their world by turning any situation into "drama." That principle accounts for each twist of events and, actually, just about any bodily gesture; on a larger scale, it constitutes a defense of the ending sequence. The other book, which rejects almost all previous critics too, lays out a "close blue-printing" along nonstridently Marxist lines. *Huckleberry Finn* becomes both an undeniably accurate picture of the Old South and a condemnation of a "profoundly corrupting and violent *milieu* in which few human virtues, such as simple loyalty to friends or respect for the lives of others," could survive. Understandably, this makes it, despite "its reputation for light and sparkle," one of the "darkest novels in American fiction," a judgment baffling to the millions who have guffawed at, say, Huck's posing as a British "valley." But insistence on Twain's political side is always useful, if only because of his genius for beguiling comedy.

During the mid-1980s, Twain watchers expected raids by the deconstructionists, but in fact they have mostly ignored his work, perhaps as too little of a challenge. For another explanation, the cutting-edge theoreticians have lately complained that Americanists are growing sluggish as a breed. Meanwhile, Twainians celebrated the centennial of *Huckleberry Finn* vigorously. Anxious for timely glitter, the mass media joined in, surely leaving an impression on some youngsters, who will show the result years later. Huck himself, who liked to remain inconspicuous as the safest way of getting along, might say that if he had "knowed what a trouble" his book would cause, he never would have written it down.

One area of criticism will have to remain an expanding mystery. No single mind can master the more than fifty languages into which *Huckleberry Finn* has been translated. Therefore, who can absorb all the prefaces, reviews, and other commentary while adjusting for a skewed text because Huck's vernacular cannot be transmuted perfectly into any other one? In fact, few Americans can handle complex ideas in Japanese alone, and perhaps no Twainian can evaluate the recent translation of *Huckleberry Finn* issued in mainland China. Even the rare English-speaking critic fluent in French and German fumbles with the other European languages and is gloomily aware that Soviet admirers have translated Twain copiously. If foreign scholar-critics often strike a native as thinly informed, the best of them raise startlingly fresh or unsettling questions. *Huckleberry Finn* needs to be related, through informed comparison rather than generalities, to other national literatures and to a truly universal perspective. Although Huck belongs to the old Mississippi Valley, his creator tried to think like one more citizen of the world.

6

This volume appears at some kind of crux in the history of criticism. Will young energy swerve in another direction, or will the thrust of innovative theories accelerate until they orbit free of all old principles? If they can, we may enter an exhilarating age of originality. Nevertheless, some of us will continue to find much learning and pleasure in the hundred years of commentary that has by now collected around *Huckleberry Finn*. Of course, whatever our reverence for settled wisdom, it is impossible to agree with every author of that commentary. But we can face up to past disagreements without abandoning criticism: *Huckleberry Finn* is so engrossing that we want to elicit its full and – some would say – changing significance. Or, rather, we want to experience it as richly as possible and must stay open to fresh interpretations, further probes toward or from the facts, and firmer ways of bringing it into our extraliterary, social dialogue.

Four fresh essays, however capable their authors, cannot synthesize the best that has been thought and said about *Huckleberry Finn* and then anticipate all the keenest insights ahead. Nor can they represent all schools of theory, and I regret that no "myth" critic appears here, for instance. This collection does avoid the most consciously avant-avant-garde: A historical scale shows that novelty based on shock value is having an increasingly short run. Furthermore, as Wayne Booth warns, we should resist "galloping neologism" because "clarity depending on new terms is at best temporary, because the new terms soon take on many new meanings in various interpretations." Still, I hope that these four essays will be perceived as aggressively open to the attitude that "we can reason together about our critical languages [and judgments], not in the sense of demonstrating that some are flatly wrong and others plainly right or true, but in the sense of probing whether they are more or less adequate to our shared experience and more or less supportive or destructive of projects in the world that we all prize."[33]

More specifically, the first essay in this collection, Michael Davitt Bell's "Mark Twain, 'Realism,' and *Huckleberry Finn,*" reexamines one of the oldest judgments about the aesthetic intention of the novel. Critics who agree on little else have praised its stunning realism. Yet Twain himself wrote surprisingly little about the purposes of fiction, and *Huckleberry Finn,* coolly observed, does not lay an ethical foundation for its antiromantic burlesque or even for Huck's growing loyalty to Jim. Grateful that Twain broke through any promulgated set of criteria and fully sensitive to his humor, Bell pinpoints the actual if shifting effects that the novel achieved. Future attempts to claim it for the party of realism will have to reckon with Bell's perspectives.

Another consensus that stretches back to 1885 is praise for the style of *Huckleberry Finn.* The convincing nature of any special line of that praise has mostly depended upon the eloquence of the critic rather than verifiable analysis. Grounded in linguistics and modern grammar, Janet Holmgren McKay's " 'An Art So High': Style in *Adventures of Huckleberry Finn*" classifies the patterns of syntax and of "errors" that characterize Huck or – thanks to his good ear – his friend Jim. In reaffirming Twain's mastery of the vernacular, she demonstrates the nuances of its social implications. She also demonstrates the dynamics of dialogue in what we too easily consider an "I" narrative. We are left far more alert to the movement from sentence to sentence, from one subtle turn of language to the next.

Lee Mitchell's " 'Nobody But Our Gang Warn't Around': The Authority of Language in *Huckleberry Finn*" also looks closely at or, rather, through the style and through Huck's assumption that words can set forth the social world, which realists believe is solidly out there. Likewise, Mitchell drives to the intellectual basis (or lack of it) for Huck's decision to help Jim. On the positive side, he accounts for the spirit of playfulness – as distinct from comedy or humor – that winds through *Huckleberry Finn,* which encourages us to believe in the possibility of inventing our own reality. Finally, he leads us to make more insightfully the distinction between Huck as a participant in the action and as a recollecting author, who in fact combines a recently illiterate boy and a mind that has some awareness of creating experience by composing a narrative.

Finally, Steven Mailloux's "Reading *Huckleberry Finn:* The Rhetoric of Performed Ideology" reaches back past McKay to the classical analyses of language as strategy. It also moves beyond the reader-response theories so influential today. Mailloux combines these approaches in order not only to identify better how humor is generated in *Huckleberry Finn* but also to enrich the debate over its topical impact within a far more socialized reality than concerns Mitchell. Like Bell, he shows how a critical judgment that attains visibility becomes part of the novel for later readers. Along with two of the other essayists, he confronts the much disputed closing sequence. Their range of positions exemplifies our current understanding of it.

7

Perhaps nobody could get at all of the astonishingly scattered writing about *Huckleberry Finn* even if a complete bibliography were available for English alone. We do have Thomas A. Tenney's magisterial, annotated, and richly indexed *Mark Twain: A Reference Guide* (1977, with annual supplements); *American Literary Scholarship/An Annual* has carried a Mark Twain chapter from its first year of coverage (for 1963); the yearly Bibliography from the Modern Language Association casts a wide yet fine net. As for a specialized listing, the last one to approach completeness appeared in the spring 1968 issue of *Modern Fiction Studies*. Although it had over 200 items, John C. Gerber commented in 1971 that a checklist of "detailed discussions" of *Huckleberry Finn* would include over 300 titles. By 1984 a survey of significant studies found thirteen book-length items and over five hundred articles and parts of books—more than for any other American novel.[34] We have to hope that someone with access to a computer intends not only to achieve up-to-date completeness but also to index the entries by key terms.

Meanwhile, the following reprintings of essays about *Huckleberry Finn* are helpful: Barry A. Marks's volume in the Problems in American Civilization Series (Boston: Heath, 1959); Kenneth S.

Lynn, *"Huckleberry Finn": Text, Sources and Criticism* (New York: Harcourt, Brace, 1961); Sculley Bradley et al., *Adventures of Huckleberry Finn* (New York: Norton Critical Edition, 1962; 2nd ed., 1977); Richard Lettis et al., *Huck Finn and His Critics* (New York: Macmillan, 1962); Claude M. Simpson in the Twentieth-Century Interpretations Series (Englewood Cliffs, N.J.: Prentice-Hall, 1968); Hamlin Hill and Walter Blair, *The Art of "Huckleberry Finn,"* 2nd ed. (San Francisco: Chandler, 1969) – includes source materials as well as a facsimile of the first edition of the novel; James K. Bowen and Richard VanDerBeets, *Adventures of Huckleberry Finn* (Glenview, Ill.: Scott, Foresman, 1970) – text of the novel "With Abstracts of Twenty Years of Criticism"; John C. Gerber, *Studies in "Huckleberry Finn"* (Columbus, Ohio: Charles E. Merrill, 1971). Also of special value, besides H. N. Smith's Riverside Edition, are Leo Marx's edition with annotations (Indianapolis: Bobbs-Merrill, 1967) and Michael Patrick Hearn, *The Annotated Huckleberry Finn* (New York: Clarkson N. Potter, 1981).

Finally, 1985 brought the hefty *One Hundred Years of "Huckleberry Finn": The Boy, His Book, and American Culture* (Columbia, Mo.: University of Missouri Press), edited by Robert Sattelmeyer and J. Donald Crowley. Its twenty-five original essays sum up past and current approaches. The editors add, in thirteen pages, a "Selective Bibliography of Criticism 1968–1983."

NOTES

1. See the Afterword (2:723) by William H. Loos in the facsimile of the manuscript (Detroit: Gale Research, 1983).
2. Jay B. Hubbell, *Who Are the Major American Writers?* (Durham, N.C.: Duke University Press, 1972), p. 139, lists other academic writers who spoke highly of Twain between 1900 and 1921. Hubbell has much interesting detail, such as the results of a poll of 400 high school and college teachers who were asked in 1926 to name 10 American "masterpieces" (pp. 289–90).
3. Both essays ran in *College English* 17 (October 1955). Since I can find no immediate cause, I must suspect an inspiring editor.
4. Walter Blair, *Mark Twain & Huck Finn* (Berkeley: University of California Press, 1960), pp. 371–84, makes some fascinating com-

parisons. Far more statistical is Robert M. Rodney, *Mark Twain International: A Bibliography and Interpretation of His Worldwide Popularity* (Westport, Conn.: Greenwood Press, 1982).

5. Frank Kermode, *The Classic: Literary Images of Permanence and Change* (New York: Viking, 1975), pp. 43–4, 130.

6. Glauco Cambon, "Mark Twain and Charlie Chaplin as Heroes of Popular Culture," *Minnesota Review* 3 (Fall 1962):77–82.

7. Barbara Herrnstein Smith, "Contingencies of Value," *Critical Inquiry* 10 (September 1983):1–35.

8. For one detailed warning see Ruth Stein, "The ABC's of Counterfeit Classics: Adapted, Bowdlerized and Condensed," *English Journal* 55 (December 1966):1160–3.

9. See especially Leland Krauth, "Mark Twain: The Victorian of Southwestern Humor," *American Literature* 54 (October 1982):368–84.

10. Doubtless the most famous reading is Leslie Fiedler's "Come Back to the Raft Agi'n, Huck Honey," *Partisan Review* 15 (June 1948):664–71. An interesting essay by Charles E. May, "Literary Masters and Masturbators: Sexuality, Fantasy, and Reality in *Huckleberry Finn,*" *Literature and Psychology* 18, no. 2 (1978):85–92, links sexual and aesthetic patterns in Twain's id.

11. See especially Hershel Parker's "Lost Authority: Non-sense, Skewed Meanings, and Intentionless Meanings," *Critical Inquiry* 9 (June 1983):767–74. The authoritative history of the composition of *Huckleberry Finn* is given in the Iowa/California Edition. The facsimile of the manuscript (1983) may be helpful.

12. Roy Harvey Pearce, " 'The End. Yours Truly, Huck Finn': Postscript," *Modern Language Notes* 24 (September 1963):253–6, speculates intriguingly and plausibly that Twain was alert to the latest territorial affairs.

13. "The Negro Writer in America: Change the Joke and Slip the Yoke," *Partisan Review* 25 (Spring 1958):212–22.

14. For an admirable analysis, see Alvin B. Kernan, *The Imaginary Library: An Essay on Literature and Society* (Princeton, N.J.: Princeton University Press, 1982).

15. In *Mark Twain: The Development of a Writer* (Cambridge, Mass.: Harvard University Press, 1962). A still more intricate discussion is found in Chapter 7, "Southwestern Vernacular," in James M. Cox, *Mark Twain: The Fate of Humor* (Princeton, N.J.: Princeton University Press, 1966), pp. 156–84.

16. My study *Our Mark Twain: The Making of His Public Personality* (Philadelphia: University of Pennsylvania Press, 1983) tries to integrate his

literary career and his development into a hero of American culture. For my view of the course of his literary reputation, see my introductions to *Critical Essays on Mark Twain, 1867–1910* (Boston: G. K. Hall, 1982), and *Critical Essays on Mark Twain, 1910–1980* (Boston: G. K. Hall, 1983).

17. Walter Slatoff, *With Respect to Readers: Dimensions of Literary Response* (Ithaca, N.Y.: Cornell University Press, 1970), p. 30. This admirable argument that literature should take primacy over the professional study of it is careful not to contradict its case with an intimidating schemata.

18. Albert E. Stone, Jr., *The Innocent Eye: Childhood in Mark Twain's Imagination* (New Haven, Conn.: Yale University Press, 1961), p. 133.

19. Reprinted, besides several other collections, in Frederick Anderson, ed., *Mark Twain: The Critical Heritage* (London: Routledge & Kegan Paul, 1971).

20. See Victor Fischer, "Huck Finn Reviewed: The Reception of *Huckleberry Finn* in the United States, 1885–1897," *American Literary Realism, 1865–1910* 16 (Spring 1983):1–57. This is a definitive work that will not be supplanted. Henry Nash Smith, "The Publication of *Huckleberry Finn*: A Centennial Retrospect," *Bulletin: The American Academy of Arts and Sciences* 37, no. 5 (February 1984):18–40, extends its significance.

21. In *Mark Twain at Work* (Cambridge, Mass.: Harvard University Press, 1942), Bernard DeVoto very influentially insisted on separating them because *Huckleberry Finn* was so evidently the greater. He complained that of forty-two critics who had recently obliged a request to name the ten leading American novels, thirty-eight "rather violently created" a book by merging the two *Adventures* (p. 87).

22. Fischer, "Huck Finn Reviewed," 37.

23. Howells's reviews and essays are gathered in *My Mark Twain* (New York: Harper's, 1910).

24. Henry Nash Smith, Introduction, *Mark Twain: A Collection of Critical Essays* (Englewood Cliffs, N.J.: Prentice-Hall, 1963), p. 1.

25. Guy A. Cardwell, "Mark Twain: The Metaphoric Hero as Battleground," *ESQ* 23 (First Quarter 1977):52–66, gives the most informed analysis of the origins, course, later shifts, and ongoing effects of the Brooks–DeVoto debate. In *A Casebook on Mark Twain's Wound* (New York: Crowell, 1962), Lewis Leary reprints the most important polemics.

26. See his later Preface to *Mark Twain at Work*, pp. vi–vii. DeVoto's most fervid generality of 1932 was foreshadowed often. For example,

William Lyon Phelps had declared that *Huckleberry Finn* "is not only the great American novel. It is America"—in *Howells, James, Bryant and Other Essays* (New York: Macmillan, 1924), p. 160.

27. Smith, Introduction, *Mark Twain: A Collection of Critical Essays*, p. 7.

28. Trilling, Introduction (New York: Rinehart, 1948). This reprinting joined a series of paperbacks widely used at the college level. Eliot's introduction (New York: Chanticleer Press, 1950) was also published in Great Britain. Thomas A. Tenney's *A Reference Guide to Mark Twain* (Boston: G. K. Hall, 1977) lists the reprintings of these and other prominent essays.

29. Philip S. Foner, *Mark Twain: Social Critic* (New York: International Publishers, 1958), p. 205. For Hoffman's comments see *Form and Fable in American Fiction* (New York: Oxford University Press, 1965); pp. 332–42; Marx's "Mr. Eliot, Mr. Trilling, and *Huckleberry Finn*" appeared first in *American Scholar* 22 (Autumn 1953):423–40.

30. Respectively, Gilbert M. Rubenstein, "The Moral Structure of *Huckleberry Finn*," *College English* 18 (November 1956):72–6; Richard P. Adams, "The Unity and Coherence of *Huckleberry Finn*," *Tulane Studies in English* 6 (1956):89–103. Both of these essays were reprinted in several collections. Smith's Riverside edition (Boston: Houghton Mifflin, 1958) belonged to another widely used series of textbooks.

31. Harold H. Kolb, Jr., "Mark Twain, Huck Finn, and Jacob Blivens: Gilt-Edged, Tree-Calf Morality in *The Adventures of Huckleberry Finn*," *Virginia Quarterly Review* 55 (Autumn 1979):653–69. For Cady, see "Huckleberry Finn in the Light of Common Day," in his *The Light of Common Day: Realism in American Fiction* (Bloomington: Indiana University Press, 1971), pp. 88–119.

32. George C. Carrington, Jr., *The Dramatic Unity of "Huckleberry Finn"* (Columbus: Ohio State University Press, 1976); Michael Egan, *Mark Twain's "Huckleberry Finn": Race, Class and Society* (Atlantic Highlands, N.J.: Humanities Press, 1977).

33. Wayne Booth, *Critical Understanding: The Powers and Limits of Pluralism* (Chicago: University of Chicago Press, 1979), p. 26; "A New Strategy for Establishing a Truly Democratic Criticism," *Daedalus* 112, no. 1 (Winter 1983):192–214.

34. Carl Dolmetsch, "*Huck Finn*'s First Century: A Bibliographical Survey," *American Studies International* 22, no. 2 (October 1984):79–121.

2

Mark Twain, "Realism," and *Huckleberry Finn*

MICHAEL DAVITT BELL

MARK Twain is one of the half-dozen or dozen major American writers, and *Adventures of Huckleberry Finn* (1884–85) is his masterpiece: On this much there is almost universal agreement. But attempt to go further, and the consensus rapidly breaks down. Given the near unanimity about Twain's stature, there is surprisingly little agreement about the nature of his achievement, about the characteristic qualities in his work that *make* him major. The terms of disagreement crystallized early in the history of Twain criticism – in Van Wyck Brooks's *The Ordeal of Mark Twain* (1920) and Bernard DeVoto's *Mark Twain's America* (1932). According to Brooks, Twain is essentially a "serious" writer, a "born, predestined artist" who was unfortunately seduced into humor by social pressure and a desire for fame. Twain's "impulse," Brooks writes, "was not that of the 'humorist'; it was that of the satirist," and "the making of the humorist was the undoing of the artist." For DeVoto, by contrast, Twain's essential quality is precisely that of the "humorist." "Clemens's earliest impulses," he writes, "led to the production of humor and nothing whatever suggests any literary impulse or desire of any other kind."[1]

Brooks's and DeVoto's positions have been considerably modified by subsequent critics, but these critics are still divided between proponents of the serious Twain – the satirist, social critic, and moralist – and proponents of Twain the humorist. Moreover, from Brooks and DeVoto to the present, critics who promote one facet of the author as essential mostly regard the opposite facet as having impeded or subverted the development of his true genius. Whereas champions of the serious Twain tend, like Brooks, to deplore any humor that cannot be explained in terms of satirical purpose,

35

champions of the humorist generally see impulses to *seriousness* as regrettable lapses.[2]

On one matter, however (in addition to Twain's major status and the centrality of *Huckleberry Finn*), these opposed critical camps seem to be in agreement: Mark Twain, they assure us, was a "realist." He was, this is to say, part of the American literary movement that supposedly, in the years after the Civil War, turned away from the "Romanticism" of the earlier nineteenth century.[3] The most outspoken proponent of the new realism, in the 1880s, was William Dean Howells, Mark Twain's closest literary friend. "Let fiction cease to lie about life," Howells proclaimed;

> let it portray men and women as they are, actuated by the motives and the passions in the measure we all know; let it leave off painting dolls and working them by springs and wires; let it show the different interests in their true proportions; let it forbear to preach pride and revenge, folly and insanity, egotism and prejudice, but frankly own these for what they are, in whatever figures and occasions they appear; let it not put on fine literary airs; let it speak the dialect, the language, that most Americans know – the language of unaffected people everywhere – and there can be no doubt of an unlimited future, not only of delightfulness but of usefulness, for it.[4]

This was the rallying cry, and Mark Twain, we have been assured again and again, was one of the new movement's most fervent and important adherents. Like Howells, so the story goes, he turned from the artifice of "springs and wires" to the portrayal of "men and women as they are." Does not the Grangerford episode in *Huckleberry Finn* show the horror of "pride and revenge"? Do not Huck's growing love and respect for Jim reveal the horror of "prejudice"? And think of Twain's development of vernacular: What other post–Civil War American novel managed better to "speak the dialect"?

As I have said, Mark Twain's "realism" is about the only quality in his work that the schools of Brooks and DeVoto can agree to praise. According to DeVoto, for example, the tradition of newspaper humor to which Twain turned at the beginning of his career "was the first vigorous realism in American literature," and "Twain's books are the culmination not only of the literature's humor but of its realism as well." According to critics of Brooks's persuasion, Twain's seriousness is fundamentally realistic, so that an innate inclination to realism is, in their view, what Twain's cultivation of humor *suppressed*. ''In addition to, and in spite of, his humorous bent,'' Theodore Dreiser wrote in 1935, Twain ''was a realist at heart''; ''in his soberer moods [he] was always the realist.''[5] Of course, the main reason DeVoto and Dreiser can agree on Twain's realism is that they mean quite different things by the term, and in this respect they are quite typical of those who have stressed Twain's connection to the tradition of American realism. For the most part, the adjective ''realistic'' has simply been attached to whatever qualities, serious or humorous, a particular critic happens to find in Twain's fiction.[6]

We have also been assured, however, that Twain *thought* of himself as a realist, that he was a realist not only in practice but in principle. After all, he was a close friend of Howells; and although *Huckleberry Finn* was published before Howells began proclaiming the new doctrine of realism (in 1886, in the ''Editor's Study'' column of *Harper's Monthly*), still the bug was in the air, and Twain must have caught it. Moreover, Twain's own pronouncements on literature – his insistence on clear writing, his attacks on ''romantic'' sloppiness – are surely the pronouncements of a realistic opponent of ''fine literary airs.'' Given the vagueness of ''realism'' as a descriptive term, at least as it has been applied to Twain, we might do well to begin with his critical writings. Just what are the ideas, it seems reasonable to ask at the outset, that emerge from these writings? And what relationship do these ideas bear to the idea of literary realism either in general or as it was expounded by Twain's close friend Howells?

It must be admitted at the start that Mark Twain's ideas about literature and fiction are more than a little difficult to fix with any certainty. His pronouncements on these matters, as on so many others, are generally so laced with irony and humor as to leave his true opinions in considerable doubt; and unlike his contemporaries, Howells and Henry James, Twain wrote little formal criticism, certainly no declaration of literary principles on the order of James's ''The Art of Fiction'' (1885) or Howells's *Criticism and Fiction* (the 1891 collection of his ''Editor's Study'' manifestos on behalf of literary realism). Instead, Twain produced a few occasional essays, pieces like "How to Tell a Story" (1894), "What Paul Bourget Thinks of Us" (1895), "Fenimore Cooper's Literary Offenses" (1895), or – to cite a rare instance of literary apprecia-tion – "William Dean Howells" (1906).[7] Mostly, Twain's literary opinions must be sifted out of his letters, his notebooks, or the much-discussed passages in his travel books and fiction burlesqu-ing or satirizing romance and the Old Masters. The first notable fact about this body of criticism is its fragmentary, incomplete, and occasional nature; unlike Howells and James, Twain apparently did not need or want to write sustained manifestos about the nature and purpose of the art of fiction. For this reason, if for no other, he stands apart from the so-called realists who rose to prominence in the 1880s.

Twain's literary opinions have been tied to realism because they seem to be based on an ingrained hostility toward romantic liter-ature, toward art or writing derived from outworn tradition and cliché rather than from observation and experience. Thus, he wrote to Howells in 1892 that Bret Harte "is as blind as a bat. He never sees anything correctly, except California scenery." Twain's favorite targets were Sir Walter Scott and James Fenimore Cooper; that the floundering steamboat in *Huckleberry Finn* is called the *Walter Scott* is, as many readers have noted, no coincidence. "Can you read [Scott] and keep your respect for him?" Twain asked Brander Matthews in a 1902 letter. "Of course a person could in *his* day – an era of sentimentality & sloppy romantics – but land! can a body do it to-day?"[8] And Cooper's "literary offenses," ac-cording to Twain, included, above all, violations of probability and failures of observation. With such overt statements in mind, critics have read much of Twain's burlesque humor – the attacks on the Old Masters in *The Innocents Abroad* (1869), the vapid sentimen-tality of Emmeline Grangerford's verses and crayon drawings in *Huckleberry Finn*, the burlesques of Malory and others in *A Connect-icut Yankeee in King Arthur's Court* (1889) – as involving, at bot-tom, a declaration of realist principle.

Such critics also point to the qualities Twain singles out for praise in works he admires. Especially notable, as an index of his preferences, are the terms in which he expressed his career-long admiration for Howells. "It is all such truth," he wrote to his

friend in 1879, praising his most recent novel, ''– truth to the life;
everywhere your pen falls it leaves a photograph''; and this metaphor keeps recurring. Of a character in another Howells novel,
Twain wrote in 1883: "You have photographed him accurately";
of one of Howells's autobiographical volumes he wrote in 1890
that it ''is perfect – perfect as the perfectest photograph the sun
ever made.''[9] The realistic ''photograph'' is apparently the proper
alternative to the clichés of Old Masters, of ''sentimentality &
sloppy romantics.''

Yet does all this, as we have so often been assured, in fact add up
to even an implicit theory of, or manifesto for, literary realism? We
should recognize, for one thing, that most of Twain's overt literary
criticism is devoted not to a discrimination of literary kinds or
modes (the novel, say, as opposed to the romance) but to a more
simple distinction between good and bad writing of whatever kind
or mode. Most of what he says about fiction smacks less of the
manifesto than of the advice manual for fledgling authors. For
instance, most of the eighteen ''rules governing literary art'' listed
in ''Fenimore Cooper's Literary Offenses'' involve strictures of this
technical variety – particularly the last seven, requiring that the
author shall:

12. *Say* what he is proposing to say, not merely come near it.
13. Use the right word, not its second cousin.
14. Eschew surplusage.
15. Not omit necessary details.
16. Avoid slovenliness of form.
17. Use good grammar.
18. Employ a simple and straightforward style.

Even the first eleven rules – calling for believable and interesting
action and character, and for dialogue resembling human speech
and consistently appropriate to the characters who speak it –
hardly depart from the genre of the practical literary handbook.[10]
All of this, of course, is good advice, but that hardly means that it
therefore constitutes an implicit theory of literary realism – or any
sort of theory at all.[11]

Twain's taste in fiction is revealed nowhere more clearly than in
a well-known letter to Howells, written in 1885– celebrated for its
opening praise of the recipient ("You are really my only author")

and for its closing, picturesque dismissal of Henry James's *The Bostonians* ("I would rather be damned to John Bunyan's heaven than read that"). What makes this letter important – and in fact a kind of touchstone of Twain's true critical principles – is the way it gets from the praise of Howells to the dismissal of James:

> You are really my only author; I am restricted to you; I wouldn't give a damn for the rest. I bored through Middlemarch during the past week, with its labored & tedious analyses of feelings & motives, & its paltry & tiresome people, its unexciting & uninteresting story, & its frequent blinding flashes of single-sentence poetry, philosophy, wit, & what-not, & nearly died from the over work. . . .
>
> Well, you have done it [that is, re-created experience; the reference is to Howells's most recent novel] with marvelous facility – & you make all the motives & feelings perfectly clear without analyzing the guts out of them, the way George Eliot does. I can't stand George Eliot, & Hawthorne & those people; I see what they are at, a hundred years before they get to it, & they just tire me to death. And as for the Bostonians, I would rather be damned to John Bunyan's heaven than read that.[12]

Except for the fact that there is less fun in it, this attack on Eliot, Hawthorne, and James has a good deal in common with the attack on Cooper published ten years later. Twain considers all of these writers, ultimately, "labored & tedious." This letter, however, is hardly a condemnation of romance by a realist; Eliot and James, at any rate, were among Howells's favorite realists. Moreover, what bothers Twain about Eliot, Hawthorne, and James – and his sense of their common ground is in fact quite perceptive – is not that they indulge in "sentimentality & sloppy romantics" but that they engage in extended psychological analysis, surely a property of a good deal of realistic fiction. The reason Twain admires Howells is that Howells *avoids* such analysis; this is the essence of his economy, his "marvelous facility."[13] Finally, and perhaps most importantly, Twain detests analysis not because it is unrealistic but because it is – to use a word dear to modern undergraduates – *boring*: "labored & tedious, ' "unexciting & uninteresting"; analytical writers "just tire me to death."

We may object to Twain's taste, but we had better recognize it for what it is. And if we simply invert his terms of condemnation, we can see clearly just what he values: "facility," economy as a relief from tedium, surprise as opposed to elaboration of the expected, clarity as opposed to complexity, characters who are "interesting" rather than "paltry & tiresome" – above all, "excitement." And if these are the values of a realist, the author of the present essay is the father of the late Dauphin. If anything, and always keeping in mind the crudeness of the celebrated distinction between the (realistic) novel and the romance, these are the values of a writer who always preferred romance – provided, of course, that it generated "interest" and "excitement" while obeying the "rules governing literary art in the realm of romantic fiction."

I am not concerned here with the question of whether Mark Twain's fiction is or is not realistic. For the moment, rather, I am concerned with the quite different question of whether the position set forth in his scattered critical writings is, as has so often been supposed, that of a realist, in any meaningful sense of that term. And my answer would be, simply: No, it is not. We also ought to note that in his occasional criticism, Twain never, in fact, uses the word "realism," not even in his letters to Howells, not even after Howells began, in 1886, to publicize the term. In an 1889 letter, Twain is full of praise for the "Editor's Study" essays, in which the campaign for realism was being conducted. "I am waiting," he writes, "to see your Study set a fashion in criticism. When that happens – as please God it must – consider that if you lived three centuries you couldn't do a more valuable work for this country, or a humaner." Here, if anywhere, one expects some comment about Howells's ideas, his ideas about the proper direction for literature. Instead, Twain proceeds to praise not the substance of Howells's "dissent" but his manner of presenting it: his "courteously reasoning" rather than "lecturing." Nor does the term "realism" appear in the appreciation of Howells's achievement Twain wrote for *Harper's* in 1906.[14]

The absence of this term from Twain's critical vocabulary, even at a time when his closest literary friend was making it the rallying cry of the American literary vanguard, ultimately has the force of a deliberate avoidance; and it seems likely that Twain avoided the term because he knew that whatever a realist was, he wasn't one. Howells, after all, consistently praised Eliot and James – and especially Jane Austen – as realists. Twain, whether he understood the term or not, just as consistently abused these very writers.[15] Perhaps, then, we ought to take him at his word – or, to speak more precisely, at his refusal to use Howells's word. Henry James subjected Howellsian realism to penetrating criticism.[16] Mark Twain – perhaps out of personal loyalty, maybe because he just didn't like abstract literary theory – never took issue with his friend's ideas. But he no more embraced these ideas than James did; he merely, it would seem, ignored them. Thus, it simply will not do, in view of all these circumstances, to imagine that Twain was a realist in principle. The case for his connection to the tradition of American realism, if it is to rest anywhere, must rest somewhere else than on the ideas expressed in his scattered critical writings.

That "somewhere else" would be, presumably, Twain's fiction. If he was not a Howellsian realist in overt principle – as he most surely was not, at least in his public and private comments on literature – was he perhaps a realist in practice, at least implicitly? I do not mean by this that his fiction might be described as realistic. It certainly might be, but the term is so flexible as to deprive such a description of any precise meaning; and, as I have already noted, the term has mainly allowed critics to describe as realistic just about any quality they happen to admire in Twain. What I mean, rather, is that we might look in the fiction for some sort of *implicit* declaration of realist principles. In his occasional criticism, as we have seen, Twain mainly abuses or ignores the preferences and principles of his friend Howells; nevertheless, it is still possible that the values at work in his novels, his criticism notwithstanding, are the values of a realist, and that *this* is what establishes his connection to the tradition of Howellsian realism. What *are* the values, then, that emerge – explicitly or implicitly – in Mark Twain's fiction? And what relationship do they bear to the main tendencies of Howells's literary doctrines? These are the questions that remain to be asked, and, since *Adventures of Huckleberry Finn* is so widely acknowledged as Twain's masterpiece, it seems appropriate to direct these questions at that book.

Realism, as Howells expounds it in the essays gathered in *Criticism and Fiction,* is less a theoretical idea than an ideological construct, having far less to do with the definition of a specific mode of literary representation than with the advocacy of ethical or political assumptions. At the center of this ideology stand two fundamental, and fundamentally related, ideas. First of all, the task of literature is defined almost wholly in moral terms; the proper role of the writer (which is what, most basically, Howellsian realism is about) is understood almost entirely in terms of his *responsibility* to his society. "The art which . . . disdains the office of teacher," Howells writes in the final paragraph of *Criticism and Fiction*, "is one of the last refuges of the aristocratic spirit which is disappearing from politics and society, and is now seeking to shelter itself in aesthetics." "Democracy in literature," he adds – and his assumptions about the political significance of realist denigration of "aethetics" are important – "is the reverse of all this."[17]

The second essential component of Howellsian realism grows directly out of the first. The realist exercises his social responsibility, first of all, by discrediting what is *irresponsible:* the "romantic," the "literary," the "artificial," the merely "artistic" – and the pervasive collocation of these terms tells us a good deal about the shape of Howells's thinking about realism. Howells repeatedly distinguishes the "literary," to its discredit, from the "human." "The supreme art in literature," he writes at the close of an admiring essay on Tolstoy, "had its highest effect in making me set art forever below humanity." "Criticism," he writes in *Criticism and Fiction*, has "put a literary consciousness into books unfelt in the early masterpieces," whereas the best work, he insists, is that in which "there is no thought of style."[18]

How relevant is all this to *Huckleberry Finn?* Deferring for the moment Howells's conception of the realist as teacher, his primary definition of the realist in terms of his social *responsibility,* his emphasis on the need to discredit the artificial or literary would seem to have an obvious and important relevance to Mark Twain and *Huckleberry Finn.* Howells himself – in *My Mark Twain,* the memoir he published in 1910 – writes in apparent admiration that "of all the literary men I have known [Clemens] was the most unliterary in his make and manner."[19] And what is more to the point, *Huckleberry Finn,* like so many of Twain's novels and travel books, is filled with burlesques of romantic or artificial art and literature.

Again and again, in the course of his journey down the Mississippi, Huck Finn encounters frauds whose addiction to outworn "style" has led to complete abandonment of common sense — and often to things much worse. Huck's story begins and ends with the efforts of Tom Sawyer, for whom "style" is everything, to bring the exoticism and excitement of romance into the mundane world of the antebellum South, and Tom is hardly unique. Emmeline Grangerford's clichéd crayon drawings and obituary verses are beautifully burlesqued; and her family's suicidal prosecution of its feud with the Shepherdsons, in the name of some dimly understood conception of honor, seems to foreshadow Howells's dire warnings about the dangers of the aristocratic spirit. So do the pretensions of the self-proclaimed Duke and Dauphin, whose butchery of Shakespeare, in the "Royal Nonesuch," once again underlines the apparent connection between outworn aristocracy and outworn style.

Huck responds to such romantic excesses with deadpan common sense. He subjects Tom's claims — that a group of children is a band of Arabs, or that genies may be summoned by rubbing lamps because "all the authorities" say so — to the test of practical experience:

> I got an old tin lamp and an iron ring and went out in the woods and rubbed and rubbed till I sweat like an Injun, calculating to build a palace and sell it; but it warn't no use, none of the genies come. So then I judged that all that stuff was only just one of Tom Sawyer's lies. I reckoned he believed in the A-rabs and the elephants, but as for me I think different. It had all the marks of a Sunday School. (HF, chap. 3)

As important as the realisms of Huck's experimental method here (or the realistic prudence of planning to sell the summoned castle) is the vernacular language in which he describes his experiment and his conclusions. "Old tin lamp," "iron ring," "sweat like an Injun," "all that stuff": Such phrases inevitably deflate the romantic discourse by which "Tom Sawyer's lies" claim to legitimize themselves.

A similar effect, to cite one more example, is produced by Huck's description of Emmeline Grangerford's sentimental drawings:

They was different from any pictures I ever see before; blacker, mostly, than is common. One was a woman in a slim black dress, belted small under the arm-pits, with bulges like a cabbage in the middle of the sleeves, and a large black scoop-shovel bonnet with a black veil, and white slim ankles crossed about with black tape, and very wee black slippers, like a chisel, and she was leaning pensive on a tombstone on her right elbow, under a weeping willow, and her other hand hanging down her side holding a white hand-kerchief and a reticule, and underneath the picture it said "Shall I Never See Thee More Alas." . . . These was all nice pictures, I reck-on, but I didn't somehow seem to take to them, because if ever I was down a little, they always give me the fan-tods. (HF, chap. 17).

Once again, the vernacular diction – "arm-pits," "like a cabbage," "like a chisel," "give me the fan-tods " – discredits Emmeline's own literary discourse.

These examples are quite typical of the antiliterary or antiro-mantic burlesque that recurs throughout *Huckleberry Finn*. Yet one might still wonder whether such burlesque necessarily serves the purposes of anything like Howellsian realism. To what extent, for instance, are Tom Sawyer's style and Emmeline Grangerford's bathetic clichés mocked for being irresponsible? Or, to put the same question in a more interesting way, to what extent does Huck's own vernacular honesty seem based on a conception of responsibility – a conception so crucial to the Howells of *Criticism and Fiction?* According to many readers of *Huckleberry Finn*, Huck's burlesques of "sentimentality & sloppy romantics" *are* ultimately based on a sense of responsibility. Huck's vernacular, in their view, is not simply a humorous device, undercutting the pretension it so neutrally describes, but a repository of positive moral value. The notion that vernacular values lie at the heart of *Huckleberry Finn* has long been central to serious readings of the novel – and es-pecially to the argument that the book's achievement is tied signif-icantly to the tradition of American realism.[20]

The problem with such readings is that they seem rather to distort Huck's own character and behavior – and even the nature of many of the targets of his humor. Although Tom Sawyer and the Duke and the Dauphin may be irresponsible, even to the point of cruelty, this is hardly the case, for instance, with Emmeline Grangerford, who is simply ridiculous. More to the point, Huck himself, while he learns to avoid cruelty to others, notably Jim, is in all other respects most characteristically irresponsible. He does not seek to change society but repeatedly flees it – to the raft, where life is "free and easy and comfortable" – or, at the close, "for the Territory ahead of the rest." And even when his voice functions as a burlesque or satirical device, Huck himself is mainly passive, seldom acknowledging in his own proper character the message implicit in his vernacular utterance. Thus Huck does not contest Tom's own belief in the "A-rabs"; his skepticism is merely personal ("but as for me I think different"). And even as he confesses his inability to "take to" Emmeline's drawings, Huck accepts the social judgment that they "was all nice pictures."

Even in Chapter 31, when Huck tears up the letter that would send Jim back into slavery, the moral importance of his decision does not take the form of anything like Howellsian responsibility. "'All right, then'" he proclaims, 'I'll *go* to hell.' . . . I shoved the whole thing out of my head; and said I would take up wickedness again, which was in my line, being brought up to it, and the other warn't" (HF, Chap. 31). Although Huck rejects the course of behavior dictated by society, he does not reject society's valuation of this behavior; his decision remains for him a form of "wickedness," just as Emmeline's drawings remain "nice pictures." Huck never, this is to say, takes overt responsibility for the moral superiority of his vernacular values; unlike the Howellsian realist he never embraces "the office of the teacher." One might object, of course, that I am making too much of Huck's irresponsibility, that I am forgetting that *Huckleberry Finn* is, after all, a work of irony and humor. But this apparent objection is really my point. The moral assumptions implicit in Huck's ironic humor (or in Twain's use of Huck for the purposes of ironic humor) are a far cry from the assumptions that form the basis of Howellsian realism.

In this connection, we might attend to the terms in which James M. Cox, in *Mark Twain: The Fate of Humor* (1966), dissents from morally serious readings of Twain's humor. Cox states quite succinctly, for instance, the point I have just been trying to make – that "since Huck's entire identity is based upon an inverted order of values . . . he cannot have any recognition of his own virtue." Cox's main argument rests on a consideration of the essential nature and function of burlesque humor, as distinguished from satire. "Criticism," he writes, "is not so much the end as the means of burlesque. The end of burlesque must be entertainment." Thus, "although much of Mark Twain's burlesque has its roots in indignation, it moves the reader not toward guilt but toward a laughter arising from recognition of the absurdity of the world; and the laughter is not an acceptance of, or a guilt toward, but a relief *from* responsibility." Turning to *Huckleberry Finn*, Cox insists that "any 'positive' value we may wish to ascribe to the experience of reading it" must depend upon the "logic of pleasure at the heart of the book" – whereas "most criticism of *Huckleberry Finn* . . . retreats from the pleasure principle toward the relative safety of 'moral issues' and the imperatives of the Northern conscience."[21] Cox's argument is inevitably oversimplifed by so brief a summary, and his approach remains controversial. It must nevertheless be recognized that an understanding of his approach at least problematizes the notion that Mark Twain's humor, in *Huckleberry Finn*, serves a serious, satirical purpose.

Cox also has some suggestive and problematic things to say about Twain's supposed realism. Twain's humor, he writes, "arises from the art of exploiting the discrepancy between futile illusion – not merely his own, but those of society and history – and 'reality.'" So far this sounds more or less compatible with Howells, but we should pay attention to the quotation marks around the key term "reality." "The humorist's creative role," Cox continues, "lay in inventing a 'reality' which would define the inadequacy of the given traditions, clichés, and illusions." In Twain's writing, as in Howells's program, reality indeed undercuts literary or romantic preconceptions; but, as Cox puts it, "the 'reality' which deflates the expectation is clearly not actuality, but an extravagant invention which, poised against the clichés, displaces them."[22] Once again, this is a far cry from the assumptions of Twain's friend Howells, for whom the essence of reality, as guarantor of social responsibility, was that it was *not* invention.

Cox's main concern is with the claims made for the serious or realistic purpose of Huck's vernacular humor, and the production of humor is not, of course, the only function of this vernacular – nor even, perhaps, its most important function. The passages in

Huckleberry Finn that one remembers and rereads with the greatest fondness are probably not those devoted to negative undercutting but those devoted to positive description and evocation. Take, for instance, the description of a river dawn that opens Chapter 19, after Huck and Jim have escaped the Grangerford–Shepherdson feud:

> Two or three days and nights went by; I reckon I might say they swum by, they slid along so quiet and smooth and lovely. . . . Not a sound, anywheres – perfectly still – just like the whole world was asleep, only sometimes the bull-frogs a-cluttering, maybe. The first thing to see, looking away over the water, was a kind of dull line – that was the woods on t'other side – you couldn't make nothing else out; then a pale place in the sky; then more paleness, spreading around; then the river softened up, away off, and warn't black any more, but gray; you could see little dark spots drifting along, ever so far away – trading scows, and such things; and long black streaks – rafts. . . .

This passage is suffused with a combination of emotional contentment and imagistic precision; it is even impressionistic, if you will, in its insistence on perception ("a kind of dull line," "little dark spots drifting along," "long black streaks") preceding objective interpretation ("the woods on t'other side," "trading scows, and such things," "rafts"). It would no doubt be plausible to describe such writing as realistic; one can certainly understand why Twain's prose in *Huckleberry Finn* mattered so much to Ernest Hemingway – who strove to get onto the page, as he put it, "the real thing, the sequence of motion and fact which made the emotion."[23] Still, this is a realism of vision, not of action; in fact, such descriptions always occur, in *Huckleberry Finn*, in moments of respite from action, moments of "comfort" when no choices need to be made. It is surely significant that Huck is most open to impressions when he is completely free of responsibility – "free and easy and comfortable on a raft." In any case, the realism of such descriptions, however we may wish to define it, has as little to do with Howellsian responsibility as does Huck's humor.

As before, then, if we wish to find some connection between the implicit values of *Huckleberry Finn* and the assumptions underlying Howellsian realism, we must continue to look elsewhere – not only beyond Twain's explicit literary opinions but beyond, as well, both the humorous and the evocative uses of vernacular in his masterpiece. The field of inquiry might seem, by now, rather hopelessly constricted, but one more area remains to be explored. Among other things, *Huckleberry Finn* is — or at least might appear to be — a novel of education, a story of its narrator's moral growth. From his complicity in the effort to defraud the Wilks girls, from his similar complicity in Tom's cruel game of ''freeing'' Jim, and especially from his own earlier discovery of his ability to care for Jim, Huck would appear to learn something about love and kindness. He would appear to grow, and *Huckleberry Finn* would appear to be the story of this growth. How, then, might we compare what Huck learns or becomes to the values associated, by Howells, with literary realism?

Early in Howells's 1890 novel, *A Hazard of New Fortunes*, the complacency of Basil and Isabel March, who are in the process of moving from Boston to New York, begins to be upset by the harsh realities of Manhattan slum life. ''The time had been,'' we are told, ''when the Marches would have taken a purely aesthetic view of the facts as they glimpsed them in this street of tenement houses, when they would have contented themselves with saying that it was as picturesque as a street in Naples or Florence and with wondering why nobody came to paint it.''[24] In the story that follows, the Marches are driven to seek some morally or politically serious alternative to their ''aesthetic view'' of urban reality. It is far from clear that either of them ever finds it, but their anxiety is important because it suggests a kind of paradigmatic plot implicit in the realist program — at least in the program of *Howellsian* realism. The protagonist would move from irresponsibly aesthetic detachment to a position of morally and politically responsible realism, making the renunciation of the aesthetic itself a kind of badge of political commitment. This admittedly ideal paradigmatic plot, with its confusion of aesthetics and politics, matters because it crops up, again and again, in the fiction of Howells's contemporaries and immediate successors, notably Frank Norris.[25] But how relevant is it, one wonders, to what happens in *Huckleberry Finn?*

One's answer would have to be that it is not very relevant at all. Huck Finn, for one thing, is not an aesthetic outsider (a status that depends as much on social class as on any specific devotion to things artistic). Rather, in terms of the realist distinction between the (genteel) aesthetic and the (lower class) real, he is an insider – part of that abstract reality that people like the Marches, for instance, can only view from a distance. Moreover, since Huck, as James Cox puts it, "cannot have any recognition of his own virtue," since he never overtly recognizes his own moral superiority, he does not share the Marches' (and Howells's) *valorization* of the real; he is no spokesman, as are so many characters in realist or naturalist fiction, for some idealized reality. Finally, Huck's confrontation with the aesthetic views or pretensions of others has little to do with the story of his development or growth, and for a fairly simple reason. Already by the end of Chapter 3, in a novel containing 43 chapters, Huck has seen through "Tom Sawyer's lies." Unlike the Marches, he has nothing left, in this respect, to learn. What leads him to continue to participate in the aesthetic games of others – notably the Duke and the Dauphin, and, in the final episode, Tom Sawyer – is not a belief in their deceptions or self-deceptions but a varying mixture of fear, humility, and loneliness.

If we wish to understand the plot or action of *Huckleberry Finn*, we need to distinguish (as serious or realist critics of the novel often fail to do) between Huck as a *device* (an ironic vehicle for Mark Twain's humor) and Huck as a *character*. And what moves Huck, the character, is neither a desire to escape a "purely aesthetic view" nor, alternatively, an impulse to expose aesthetic frauds. His primary motives are more personal and human, which is one of the reasons *Huckleberry Finn* is a masterpiece. Take, for instance, Huck's account of his reasons for participating in what he sees to be the ridiculous schemes of Tom Sawyer's gang. He recognizes that their "swords" are "only lath and broom-sticks," and he does not believe, in any case, that "we could lick such a crowd of Spaniards and A-rabs." "But," he adds, "I wanted to see the camels and elephants, so I was on hand next day" (HF, chap. 3). Huck, this is to say, is *curious*. So, too, when Huck and Jim approach the sinking *Walter Scott*, Huck insists on boarding her, against Jim's strenuous objections. "I wanted to get aboard of her,'' he explains, ''and slink around a little, and see what was there'' (HF, chap. 12).

Huck soon mounts another argument for boarding the *Walter Scott*. ''Do you reckon,'' he asks Jim, ''Tom Sawyer would ever go by this thing?'' (HF, chap. 12). Again and again, to the dismay of serious readers, Huck seems to accept Tom's values – finally, at the Phelps farm, even taking on Tom's name. Why, we have often asked, does Huck repeatedly adopt values he dismissed at the outset as lies? One answer would be that values (in the sense of the realist distinction between the falsely literary and the genuinely human or real) do not lie at the heart of Huck's story. Another answer appears in the book's opening chapter, and suggests that behind even Huck's curiosity is a far deeper feeling. He is alone at night, in his room at Miss Watson's. ''I set down in a chair by the window,'' Huck writes, ''and tried to think of something cheerful, but it warn't no use. I felt so lonesome I most wished I was dead. . . . I got so down-hearted and scared, I did wish I had some company.'' It is at precisely this moment that Huck hears something ''stirring'' beneath his window. ''I put out the light,'' he writes, ''and scrambled out of the window onto the shed. Then I slipped down to the ground and crawled in amongst the trees, and sure enough there was Tom Sawyer waiting for me'' (HF, chap. 1). Huck's reason for joining Tom, in other words, is that he is lonely and frightened, that he wants distraction, companionship, friendship – ultimately, of course, love.

Jim, on Jackson's Island, becomes Huck's replacement for Tom Sawyer. ''I was ever so glad to see Jim,'' Huck writes. ''I warn't lonesome, now'' (HF, chap. 8). And if Huck grows during the course of his story, it is not because he is educated in reality (as opposed to the falsely aesthetic) but because he discovers, with Jim, the possibility of a love deeper than the distraction offered by Tom Sawyer's gang. This love involves responsibility, to be sure, but it is *personal* responsibility, not the sort of abstract *social* responsibility Howells would call for in *Criticism and Fiction*. Huck learns about this kind of responsibility when he betrays Jim's confidence – when he puts a dead snake in Jim's bed in Chapter 10 or when he pretends they were never separated by the fog in Chapter 15.

He learns even more from the moments, in Chapter 16 and Chapter 31, when he determines *not* to betray Jim. We might want to question the depth of Huck's love for Jim; he often seems to forget about him, for instance, when Jim is absent or presumed dead, as in the beginning of the Grangerford episode in Chapter 17. But what matters most for our present purposes is that we recognize how little the story of Huck's growth in personal loyalty to Jim has to do with the assumptions of Howellsian realism, or with the paradigmatic plot or action implicit in these assumptions.

The problem of the ending of *Huckleberry Finn*, quite simply, is that what happens at the Phelps farm seems to turn away from, or even to undermine, what Huck has experienced with Jim. Huck's participation in Tom's cruel "evasion" seems an inexplicable betrayal of what Huck has already twice decided *not* to betray: his personal responsibility to Jim. I have no wish, here, to enter into the debate about whether the ending of *Huckleberry Finn* is or is not appropriate.[26] But the dissatisfaction the ending has aroused in readers does indicate, once again, how irrelevant the tradition of American realism is to the achievement of Twain's novel. It is a nice paradox that the ending perhaps especially troubles serious and realist readers, for what happens in the final episode would seem to be what they are looking for. Huck the human character is displaced once again by Huck the humorous device, and it is on Huck's function as a device — on a serious, satirical reading of the novel's antiliterary burlesques — that the case for its realism is most often based; and what *is* this final episode if not a sustained (perhaps oversustained) antiliterary burlesque? That realist readers have nevertheless found the ending of *Huckleberry Finn* disappointing thus suggests that even *their* deepest response to the book has litle to do with its supposed realism, its burlesque of the romantic and literary. When Twain reverts, or seems to revert, to the distinction between life and literature, they, too, miss his earlier powerful evocation of loneliness and love.

My overall point, in this essay, is that the case for the connection of *Huckleberry Finn* to the tradition of American realism seems, at virtually every point, an exceptionally weak one, whether one is considering Twain's literary ideas, the function of burlesque humor in the novel, or the book's plot or action. It might be objected, even granting this point, that making the point at all appears to involve one in a curiously negative critical enterprise. Arguments about what *did* influence a writer, although they have a clear purpose, are often rather dry and pedantic. To argue about what did *not* influence a writer might seem like maintaining the pedantic dryness while sacrificing the purpose. But there are in fact at least three lessons to be learned from recognizing the tenuousness of *Huckleberry Finn*'s relationship to the realistic tradition of which William Dean Howells was so fervent a spokesman.

For one thing, this recognition might allow us to see American literary history a little more clearly – as something more complicated (and more interesting) than a series of more or less homogenized, generational "movements." Surely a term like "realist" ought to indicate something more important than the general dates of an author's career. Recognizing the fundamental irrelevance of Howellsian realism to *Huckleberry Finn* might also help us to understand the specific achievement of this novel more clearly. In part, to be sure, this too is a rather negative enterprise, like clearing away a tangle of accumulated preconception and misconception without ever quite getting to the positive task of exploring and appreciating the revealed terrain. Still, even this apparently negative enterprise has, in and of itself, a positive side. To recognize the qualities in *Huckleberry Finn* – in its humor, its language, and its human action – that distinguish it from the dogmas of realism is already, after all, to describe some of the very qualities that make it the special sort of book it is.

The third lesson to be learned by disconnecting *Huckleberry Finn* from Howellsian realism has to do with the possibility thereby offered of gaining a more precise understanding of Mark Twain's development as a writer – and of the relationship of this development to the literary movements of Twain's time. For it is not quite enough, in this context, simply to say that Twain was not a realist and to leave it at that. Twain never, as I have already noted, used the terms "realist" and "realism," but Howells was his close friend, and Twain did read the "Editor's Study" essays faithfully, from the time they began appearing in 1886. And Howells's ideas, however irrelevant they may be to *Huckleberry Finn,* would seem to have influenced the first novel Twain published after Howells began his campaign for literary realism. I refer, of course, to *A Connecticut Yankee in King Arthur's Court*, which appeared in 1889. Twain's Yankee, unlike Huck Finn, repeatedly insists on the moral and political superiority of his own values; he openly attacks the romantic and literary; and he associates this attack, quite explicitly, with political reform. Is it any wonder that Howells, who thought *A Connecticut Yankee* the greatest of Twain's works, called it "an object-lesson in democracy"?[27]

Many reasons have been proposed for the transformation in Twain's writing, generally regarded as a decline, between *Huckleberry Finn* and *A Connecticut Yankee*.[28] Although I have no space to rehearse these explanations here, I offer the speculation that the influence of Howellsian realism may have played its part in Twain's transformation. For in *A Connecticut Yankee*, as distinguished from *Huckleberry Finn*, Howells's ideas about the political significance of antiliterary satire and about the general nature and purpose of serious literature do seem to be important – and their importance seems generally to have been unfortunate. But that is another story. For the moment, we might simply reflect that the distance between *Huckleberry Finn* and the tradition of American realism is not merely a pedantic bit of information to be filed in the dry databasement of literary history. It is also, perhaps, something for which lovers of Twain's masterpiece should be grateful.

NOTES

1. Van Wyck Brooks, *The Ordeal of Mark Twain* (New York: Dutton, 1920), pp. 31, 208, 218; Bernard DeVoto, *Mark Twain's America and Mark Twain at Work* (Boston: Houghton Mifflin, 1967), p. 101.
2. The *locus classicus* of the stand-off between proponents of the humorous and serious Twains is the famous debate about the ending of *Huckleberry Finn*, beginning with Ernest Hemingway's declaration that "if you read it you must stop where the Nigger Jim is stolen from the boys. This is the real end. The rest is just cheating" (*Green Hills of Africa* [New York: Scribner's, 1935], p. 22). Leo Marx argues that the burlesque ending betrays the serious implications of the novel in "Mr. Eliot, Mr. Trilling, and *Huckleberry Finn*," *American Scholar* 22 (1953): 423–40.

His targets, on the basis of equally serious readings of the novel, *defend* the ending. See Lionel Trilling, *"Huckleberry Finn,"* in *The Liberal Imagination* (New York: Scribner's, 1950), pp. 104–17, and T. S. Eliot, Introduction to *Huckleberry Finn* (1950), reprinted in Claude M. Simpson, ed., *Twentieth Century Interpretations of Huckleberry Finn* (Englewood Cliffs, N.J.: Prentice-Hall, 1968), pp. 107–8. James Cox, to continue the available permutations and combinations, *defends* the ending as part of his *attack* on serious readings of the book. See *Mark Twain: The Fate of Humor* (Princeton, N.J.: Princeton University Press, 1966), pp. 175–82. For a more recent and extremely provocative reading of the ending, see Laurence B. Holland, "A 'Raft of Trouble': Word and Deed in *Huckleberry Finn,*" in Eric J. Sundquist, ed., *American Realism: New Essays* (Baltimore: John Hopkins University Press, 1982), pp. 66–81. And for a general discussion of this debate, see John Reichert, *Making Sense of Literature* (Chicago: University of Chicago Press, 1977), pp. 191–203.

3. The commonplace that the story of American fiction in the years following the Civil War is the story of the rise of realism is so widespread as to defy citation, but its currency is indicated, for instance, by the frequency with which the term "realism" appears in the titles and subtitles of books dealing with post–Civil War American literature. See, for example, Vernon Louis Parrington, *The Beginnings of Critical Realism in America, 1860–1920*, Vol. 3 of *Main Currents of American Thought* (New York: Harcourt, Brace, 1930); Everett Carter, *Howells and the Age of Realism* (Philadelphia: Lippincott, 1954); Warner Berthoff, *The Ferment of Realism: American Literature: 1864–1919* (New York: Free Press, 1965); Harold H. Kolb, Jr., *The Illusion of Life: American Realism as a Literary Form* (Charlottesville: University Press of Virginia, 1969); Edwin H. Cady, *The Light of Common Day: Realism in American Fiction* (Bloomington: Indiana University Press, 1971); Chapter 6, "Fictions of the Real," in Alan Trachtenberg, *The Incorporation of America: Culture and Society in the Gilded Age* (New York: Hill and Wang, 1982), pp. 182–207; and Sundquist, ed., *American Realism: New Essays*.

4. William Dean Howells, *Criticism and Fiction* (1891), in Clara Marburg Kirk and Rudolf Kirk, eds., *Criticism and Fiction and Other Essays by W. D. Howells* (New York: New York University Press, 1959), p. 51.

5. DeVoto, *Mark Twain's America*, pp. 91, 257; Theodore Dreiser, "Mark the Double Twain," *English Journal* 24 (1935):622, 623.

6. At times, for instance, DeVoto simply seems to equate realism with Western Americanism as opposed to Eastern intellectualism. Twain,

he writes in this vein, "was untutored; his only discipline was reality": or note DeVoto's dismissal of "literary criticism" on the grounds that "that department of beautiful thinking is too insulated from reality for my taste" (*Mark Twain's America*, pp. 194, xii). For a more recent example of the tendency to apply the term "realism" to whatever quality a reader happens to find in Twain, one might look at Kolb's *The Illusion of Life: American Realism as a Literary Form*. Twain, Kolb writes, shared with James and Howells "the instinct for the antiomniscient point of view" (p. 68) – which is no doubt true, but which hardly therefore distinguishes Twain, as a realist, from such supposed romancers as, for instance, Charles Brockden Brown, Edgar Allan Poe, or Herman Melville. Nor, to cite one more example, does the fact that Twain's characters "tend to have mixed motives and confused consciences" (p. 110) seem in any obvious way to distinguish Twain as a realist.

7. "How to Tell a Story" (*Youth's Companion*, 1894), reprinted in Justin Kaplan, ed., *Great Short Works of Mark Twain* (New York: Harper & Row, 1967), pp. 182–7; "What Paul Bourget Thinks of Us" (*North American, Review*, 1895), in *How to Tell a Story and Other Essays* (Hartford, Conn.: American Publishing Co., 1900), pp. 141–64; "Fenimore Cooper's Literary Offenses" (*North American Review*, 1895), reprinted in Kaplan, ed., *Great Short Works*, pp. 169–81; "William Dean Howells," *Harper's Monthly* 113 (1906):221–5. For a portion of the Cooper essay deleted from the published version, see Bernard DeVoto, "Fenimore Cooper's Further Literary Offenses," *New England Quarterly* 19 (1946):291–301.

8. *Mark Twain–Howells Letters: The Correspondence of Samuel L. Clemens and William Dean Howells, 1872–1910*, ed. Henry Nash Smith and William M. Gibson (Cambridge, Mass,: Harvard University Press, 1960), p. 396; letter to Matthews quoted in Albert Bigelow Paine, *Mark Twain: A Biography* (New York: Harper's 1912), p. 1197.

9. Smith and Gibson, eds., *Mark Twain–Howells Letters*, pp. 245, 427, 633.

10. Kaplan, ed., *Great Short Works*, pp. 169–71.

11. Everett Carter, summarizing "Fenimore Cooper's Literary Offenses," asserts that "the rules governing literary art, Twain made it clear, should be the rules of the realist" (*Howells and the Age of Realism*, p. 72). Yet Richard Chase's summary of the essay seems more convincing. "This is not," he writes, "an attempt to demolish romance and substitute realism. On the contrary, despite its negative approach, Mark Twain's essay is intended to show how romance must be writ-

56

ten. He is lecturing Cooper on the 'rules governing literary art in the domain of romantic fiction.' He is pleading not for realism as such but for realism as the only way of effectively assimilating the miraculous'' (*The American Novel and Its Tradition* [Garden City, N.Y.: Doubleday, 1957], pp. 147–8).

12. Smith and Gibson, eds., *Mark Twain–Howells Letters*, p. 534.

13. Howells appreciated this insight. ''What people cannot see,'' he complained in his reply to Twain's letter, ''is that I analyze as little as possible, but go on talking about the analytical school – which I am suppose[d] to belong to; and I want to thank you for using your eyes'' (Smith and Gibson, eds., *Mark Twain–Howells Letters*, pp. 535–6).

14. Ibid., p. 613; ''William Dean Howells,'' *Harper's Monthly* 113 (1906): 221–5.

15. ''Realism,'' Howells wrote ''is nothing more and nothing less than the truthful treatment of material, and Jane Austen was the first and the last of the English novelists to treat material with entire truthfulness'' (Kirk and Kirk, eds., *Criticism and Fiction and Other Essays*, p. 38). Twain's attacks on Jane Austen are notorious. Especially picturesque is the comment in a 1909 letter to Howells: ''Jane is entirely impossible. It seems a great pity they allowed her to die a natural death'' (Smith and Gibson, eds., *Mark Twain–Howells Letters*, p. 841).

16. See James, ''William Dean Howells,'' *Harper's Weekly* 30 (1886):394–5.

17. Kirk and Kirk, eds., *Criticism and Fiction*, p. 87. Howells's definition of the writer's role in terms of his social function and obligation persists in the critical writing of Frank Norris, and can be seen, for instance, in the essay title that also became the title of the posthumous collection of his critical essays: ''The Responsibilities of the Novelist.'' See *The Complete Works of Frank Norris*, vol. 7 (Garden City, N.Y.: Doubleday, 1928). I have discussed the connections between Howells's and Norris's literary ideas in ''Frank Norris, Style, and the Problem of American Naturalism,'' *Studies in the Literary Imagination* 16, no. 2 (Fall 1983):93–106.

18. William Dean Howells, *My Literary Passions* (New York: Harper & Brothers, 1895), p. 258; Howells, *Criticism and Fiction*, p. 26. I discuss the assumptions underlying Howellsian realism at far greater length in ''The Sin of Art and the Problem of American Realism: William Dean Howells,'' *Prospects* 9 (1985):115–42.

19. *Literary Friends and Acquaintance*, ed. David F. Hiatt and Edwin H. Cady (Bloomington: Indiana University Press, 1968), p. 266.

20. See especially, in this regard, Kenneth S. Lynn, *Mark Twain and*

Southwestern Humor (Boston: Little, Brown, 1960), and Henry Nash Smith, *Mark Twain: The Development of a Writer* (Cambridge, Mass.: Harvard University Press, 1962).

21. Cox, *Mark Twain: The Fate of Humor*, pp. 172, 44, 179.

22. Ibid., pp. 12, 47.

23. Ernest Hemingway, *Death in the Afternoon* (New York: Charles Scribner's Sons, 1932), p. 2.

24. William Dean Howells, *A Hazard of New Fortunes* (New York: New American Library, 1965), p. 65.

25. One thinks particularly here of the education of the Eastern poet, Presley, in Norris's *The Octopus* (1901), and of the melodramatic growth to real manhood of the effete socialite, Ross Wilbur, in Norris's *Moran of the Lady Letty* (1898). As the latter example suggests, the paradigmatic realist plot shades over rapidly into the tale of atavistic "Darwinian" reversion (from effete civilization to "real," instinctive bestiality) produced again and again by so-called American naturalists – Norris's *McTeague* (1899) and *Vandover and the Brute* (1914, posthumous) or Jack London's *The Call of the Wild* (1903) and *The Sea Wolf* (1904). In the work of Stephen Crane, however, notably in his New York City sketches, the Howellsian issue of perspective – of the educated outsider seeking to understand the reality of urban slum dwellers – remains paramount, and Crane was generally more aware than Howells of the corruption and confusion involved in the middle-class association of poverty with reality. For an excellent discussion of this aspect of Crane's work, see Alan Trachtenberg, "Experiments in Another Country: Stephen Crane's City Sketches," in Sundquist, ed., *American Realism: New Essays*, pp. 138–54.

26. For a description of this critical debate, see note 2 above.

27. *Harper's Monthly*, 80 (January 1890):320.

28. Henry Nash Smith, for instance, argues that Twain, in *A Connecticut Yankee*, "was subjecting the vernacular perspective . . . to a test that destroyed it. He tried not merely to transform the vernacular value system into a political ideology, but to make it the conceptual framework for a novel embodying his philosophy of history and using this framework to interpret nineteenth-century civilization" (Smith *Mark Twain: The Development of a Writer*, p. 138). Smith returned to the problems of *A Connecticut Yankee* in *Mark Twain's Fable of Progress* (New Brunswick, N.J.: Rutgers University Press, 1964). According to James Cox, on the other hand, *A Connecticut Yankee* employs not "vernacular" but "slang," and the movement from vernacular to

slang lies at the heart of the book's failure. "Doubting his burlesque impulse," Cox adds, "Mark Twain had tried to make his book serious; determining to write a satire, he had destroyed his humorous genius; seeking for truth and ideology, he deserted the pleasure principle" (*Mark Twain: The Fate of Humor*, pp. 219, 224).

3

"An Art So High": Style in
Adventures of Huckleberry Finn

JANET HOLMGREN MCKAY

*A*DVENTURES *of Huckleberry Finn* has been praised over the one
hundred years of its existence for its remarkable originality.
The publication of Twain's most widely read and accomplished
novel was, as one critic recently put it, "an event incalculably
important to the development of a genuinely American literature."[1] That critic goes on to make a very important point about
the novel's significance: "That the novel played a central role in
the liberation of American literature is beyond dispute; but it is
also, at a perhaps less exalted but more immediately recognizable
level, a book that has brought unbounded delight to more people
than can be imagined."[2] I am reminded of the comment of a
student recently who complained that the "learned" footnotes in
the Norton critical edition "gave away the ending." Those of us
who have a long familiarity with and love for the novel sometimes
forget that it still has the power to delight new readers.

After one hundred years, *Huckleberry Finn* still impresses old and
new friends with the profound moral truths that the innocent
Huck discovers in his quest to be free and comfortable. The novel
still delights us with its unforgettable characters and with its hon-
est, unvarnished picture of rural American life before the Civil
War. It still makes readers laugh out loud and feel deeply for Huck
and Jim. And it still kindles in many of us a longing to experience
firsthand the beauty of the great Mississippi River. For these and
many other reasons, the novel ranks among the greatest works in
Western literature.

Underlying and augmenting all of its many attributes is the language of *Huckleberry Finn* – prose that changed the voice of American literature, prose that strikes readers as fresh and as exciting

now as it did in 1885. I believe that to understand the significance of this novel – to understand the pleasure we derive from it and the source of its extraordinary success – we must look into the complexity, sophistication, and innovation of its style. So much has been said about this style that it may be foolhardy to tackle it again, but each time I approach it from a new perspective, I come away with a deeper appreciation for its power.

There is something so special and ingenuous about the style that one can readily agree with Albert Stone when he says that "the vernacular language . . . in *Huckleberry Finn* strikes the ear with the freshness of a real boy talking out loud."[3] Stone's comment hits home on several counts. First, this style does "strike the ear" – we hear it as we read it – and that quality, coupled with its colloquialness, creates the illusion of talk. Second, because of the way Twain controls both the language and the point of view, we are struck over and over again with how true the story is to the boy who tells it.

Tony Tanner notes that "from the start of his writing career, Clemens reveals a preoccupation with language problems."[4] Twain's interest in language started with his lifelong love of good talk. His constant preoccupation with the artful fictions of platform speaking, in which certain artificial hesitations and pauses added to the apparent naturalness of the delivery,[5] led him to try to capture these variations of speech in writing. Louis J. Budd does not exaggerate when he stresses Twain's commitment to "talk": "Even after he was established as a leading author he would analyze oral performance much more consciously and astutely than the craft of writing."[6]

Twain's respect for and understanding of the spoken word and its power of expression led him to try to capture some of its qualities in his written style and in his presentation of all types of discourse. To ensure the authenticity of dialect in written form, he went through the painstaking process of "talking and talking and *talking* till it sounds right."[7] He applied his standards for oral presentations to written works by subjecting them to "the most exacting of tests – the reading aloud."[8]

Four years after completing *Huckleberry Finn*, Twain explored the complex relationship between spoken and written language in a note to an interviewer, Edward Bok:

> Spoken speech is one thing, written speech is quite another . . . The moment "talk" is put into print you recognize that it is not what it was when you heard it; you perceive that an immense something has disappeared from it. That is its very soul. . . . To add interpretations [to talk] which would convey the right meaning is a something which would require – what? An art so high and fine and difficult that no possessor of it would ever be allowed to waste it on interviews.[9]

It is this art, this ability to maintain the semblance of talk in written form while at the same time investing it with the spirit and animation of the speaker, that informs and controls the narrative of *Huckleberry Finn*.

Twain attempted, through his style in *Huckleberry Finn*, to give expression to what Henry Nash Smith calls the vernacular values of "homely wisdom and rugged honesty that were an implicit indictment of empty elegance and refinement."[10] For Twain, style, the way in which an idea is expressed, was inextricably linked to the character of the observer. Style in language was a reflection of the speaker's personality and mode of perception.

Twain drew on two sources for vernacular models. His primary inspiration was the oral tradition of the frontier – the boastful bombast of the tall-tale teller and the plain, understated style of the simple, uneducated American. In addition, he frequently praised the naive qualities in young people's writing. He saw the fresh perceptivity of children mirrored in their composition. Thus, he says in his "Complaint about Correspondents," "the most . . . interesting letters we get here from home are from children seven and eight years old. . . . They write simply and naturally, and without straining for effect."[11] In his "Autobiography" he takes pleasure in quoting lengthy passages from his daughter Susy's biography of him.

In Huck Finn, Twain created a narrator with a boy's innocence and a social outcast's honesty. He achieved this effect with certain vernacular features, such as nonstandard verb forms, a limited vocabulary, and apparently simple syntactic relations, while building into the style a highly sophisticated, innovative literary voice that stretches the English language to its limits and draws on a wide variety of poetic devices. Huck's limitations as a narrator enabled Twain to experiment freely with the range of expressiveness inherent in the colloquial style without the necessity of doctoring it to meet standard literary expectations.

The kinds of errors that Huck makes are by no means haphazard; Twain carefully placed them to suggest Huck's basic illiteracy but not to overwhelm the reader. Nonstandard verb forms constitute Huck's most typical mistakes. He often uses the present form or past participle for the simple past tense, for example, *see* or *seen* for *saw*; his verbs frequently do not agree with their subjects in number and person; and he often shifts tense within the same sequence.

On the most obvious level, Huck's frequent substitution of present for preterit is typical both of nonstandard English and of conversation in general. In another sense, Huck's present tense takes his experiences and generalizes them to the habitual present,[12] as when, in describing a typical Mississippi sunrise, he tells the reader, "you see the mist curl up off of the water, and the east reddens up, and you make out a log cabin in the edge of the woods" (HF, Chap. 19).

In a similar way, Huck frequently uses the modals *could* and *would* in his descriptions of nature. Thus, in that same "Sunrise on the River" description at the beginning of Chapter 19, Huck tells the reader what "you could see" and "you could hear." The *could* preterits, suggesting repeated activity, coupled with the impersonal *you*, generalize the response and imply the unstated condition – "whenever you were there or whenever the sun rose." When Huck describes the summer storm he and Jim watch on Jackson's Island, he starts in the simple past tense and then says: "It *would* get so dark that it looked all blue-black outside . . . and the rain *would* thrash along . . . and here *would* come a blast of wind that *would* bend the trees down" (Chap. 9; italics are added). These *would* constructions suggest repeated actions and events and create a generalized sense of the past.

Huck's present tense also identifies his involvement in the process of storytelling. He uses what Martin Joos calls "the narrative actual present" that "has a firm basis in speech, where the use of actual tense for past events comes naturally to the lips of a man who gets himself involved in what he is talking about."[13] Thus, Huck tells us that "the king gets up and comes forward a little" or "the king begins to work his jaw again" (HF, Chap. 25).

Finally, Huck uses the timeless present[14] to frame his moral judgments or his comments and generalizations: "Music *is* a good thing"; "Human beings *can* be awful cruel to one another." Except for these gnomic statements, Huck does not use the present tense to step out of his narrative and offer retrospective evaluations of the events of the story. Only in the opening and closing paragraphs does he discuss his narrative function: "You don't know about me . . ."; "Tom's most well, now . . . so there ain't nothing more to write about."

Huck's choice of verbs is both colloquial and concrete. His verbs are active and direct, as are those of other characters. In Huck's world it doesn't get dark, it "darkens up"; *Tom Sawyer* doesn't end, it "winds up." When the King gets caught in a big lie at the Wilkses, he doesn't turn white but he "whitened." Huck frequently "lights out" and "strikes" home, town, or the raft. When he is on the run, he "humps" it to get away. Many of these active verbs are two part – verb plus adverbial particle – "soften up," "tie up," "set out," "lay up," "drift along," "blubber out." These constructions are especially common in American English; they lend a colloquial quality to the prose while at the same time adding to the rhythm.

While Huck's vocabulary is rich in concrete finite verbs (they average 15 percent of the text, in contrast to 5 percent for adjectives), participial verb forms fulfill an important role as modifiers. Huck's frequent use of present participles as postnominal adjectives adds to the rhythm of his style. Thus, for example, in the sunrise passage, the reader shares the vision of "the paleness, spreading around" and "dark spots drifting along." Frequently, Twain adds the colloquial "a-" prefix to Huck's present participles, and he couples these forms with two-syllable adverbials for even greater rhythm. During the thunderstorm, Huck glimpses "tree-tops a-plunging about, away off yonder." At the circus, the bare-back riders go "a-weaving around the ring" (HF, Chap. 22). When

Huck recalls the highlights of their trip, he remembers Jim and him "a floating along, talking, and singing, and laughing" (HF, Chap. 31).

In addition to the nonstandard verb forms, Twain establishes Huck's basic illiteracy with a series of strategically placed errors. Huck uses certain dialect terms in place of more standard choices, *without* for *unless* or *except,* for example. Huck confuses some similar-sounding words, such as *diseased* for *deceased,* and he shares this confusion with other characters. The King regularly mixes up terms, such as his substitution of *orgies* for *obsequies.* In some cases, it is impossible to tell whether a mistake is Huck's or simply his naive report of someone else's mistake. In this regard, Twain occasionally has Huck use a dialect spelling, which sometimes reflects a dialect pronunciation, as with *deffersit* for *deficit,* and sometimes just a misspelling, as with *sivilize.* Huck keeps his distance by misspelling alien forms, and the reader recognizes them as someone else's words and sentiments.

Although the dialect forms stand out, Robert Lowenherz calculates that Twain restricted "dialect spelling to less than one percent of Huck's narrative speech . . . consistently throughout the novel."[15] Similarly, in revising *Huckleberry Finn,* Twain introduced many nonstandard features in strategic places while regularizing the grammar at other points, so that the dialect and suggestions of illiterate usage "might count."[16] Among those nonstandard features, the most prominent other than the verb forms are the frequent occurrence of double negatives, the use of adjectives for adverbs, and a redundancy of subjects – for example, "Aunt Sally she's going to adopt me." Huck's double negatives frequently have a literary effect. For example, in the first paragraph of the novel, Huck's "but that ain't no matter" characterizes him as both illiterate and self-effacing.

On the surface, Huck's syntactic patterns appear simple, but they are more complex than they seem. Twain does not adopt the childish and boring pattern of having one simple sentence follow another. In fact, Huck's sentences are not particularly short, except for an occasional matter-of-fact evaluation ("She was right about the rats," "The seegars was prime," "The statements was interesting, but tough"). Nor do Huck's sentences lack complexity, but they are made to seem simple by a lack of overt indications of subordination between clauses and phrases. For example, Huck characteristically uses the conjunction *and* to link any number of subordinate and coordinate ideas, a practice that suggests a lack of linguistic sophistication.

So, for example, in a sentence in which Huck describes his intense activities as he engineers his escape from Pap, the relationship among the predicates depends upon the narrative sequence – one activity follows another: "Well, *next* I took an old sack *and* put a lot of rocks in it, – all I could drag – *and* I started it from the pig, *and* dragged it to the door *and* through the woods down to the river *and* dumped it in, *and* down it sunk, out of sight" (HF, Chap. 7; italics added). Prepositional phrases locate the action, add rhythm, and break up the repetition of verbs linked by *and*. The juxtaposition of the adverbial particle before the subject and verb in "down it sunk" (by contrast with "dumped it in") breaks the pattern of the other predicates and adds a note of finality.

When Huck describes a scene rather than a series of activities or events, the relationship among parts of sentences is even looser. Frequently, however, there is still the connection based upon time within the narrative sequence. As the sun rises on the Mississippi, "The first thing to see . . . was a kind of dull line . . . then a pale place in the sky; then more paleness spreading around; then the river softened up. . . ." The semicolon recurs as regularly as *and* to establish loose connections.

Huck's more complex sentences are not difficult to understand, because he uses simple sequencing to link ideas together. Thus, a sentence describing the circus contains a series of sophisticated absolutes – participial phrases with subjects – as well as other modifiers, but it reads like one impression naturally following another: "And then one by one they got up and stood, and went a-weaving around the ring so gentle and wavy and graceful, the men looking ever so tall and airy and straight, with their heads bobbing and skimming along, away up there under the tent-roof, and every lady's rose-leafy dress flapping soft and silky around her hips, and she looking like the most loveliest parasol" (HF, Chap. 22). As Richard Bridgman notes, "Huck's remembering mind lays in these

67

details one after the other without any urge toward subordination."[17]

This sentence incorporates another of Huck's typical syntactic patterns. When he uses a string of three adjectives, he frequently uses *and* and occasionally *or* ("the watermelons, or the cantelopes, or the mushmelons, or what") after each one. This practice accords each idea equal weight while at the same time adding to the rhythm.

With Huck's apparently simple syntax, Twain is able to produce some remarkable effects. In one of the novel's most interesting passages, Twain has Huck report one of the King's performances by summarizing part and giving part verbatim. In a single sentence, Huck sets the scene, records the speech, and offers an evaluation.

> Well, by and by the king he gets up and comes forward a little, and works himself up and slobbers out a speech, all full of tears and flapdoodle about its being a sore trial for him and his poor brother to lose the diseased, and to miss seeing diseased alive, after the long journey of four thousand mile, but it's a trial that's sweetened and sanctified to us by this dear sympathy and these holy tears, and so he thanks them out of his heart and out of his brother's heart, because out of their mouths they can't, words being too weak and cold, and all that kind of rot and slush, till it was just sickening; and then he blubbers out a pious goody-goody Amen, and turns himself loose and goes to crying fit to bust.[18]

Huck's narration frames his account of the King's speech. Twain begins with Huck's introduction, moves into Huck's rendition of the King's words ("its being a sore trial for him and his brother"), and finally, in the middle of the sentence, gives us the King himself speaking ("it's a trial that's sweetened and sanctified to us"). From this point on, we move gradually back to Huck's voice, passing once again through the intermediate stage of Huck's account of the King ("because out of their mouths they can't").

The large number of loosely coordinated clauses, the repetition of certain phrases ("by and by") to link sentences together, occasional ambiguity or vagueness about a pronominal referent, occasional sentence ellipsis, variable sentence length, and a wide range of verb tenses and aspects all contribute to the "colloquialness" of the Huck Finn style. It is, however, probably Huck's vocabulary above all else that "strikes the reader's ear." Huck's limited vocabulary depends for its power on strategic repetition, the coining of new terms, and the expansion of traditional functions for words.

Huck repeats certain key words, such as *monstrous, lonesome,* and *comfortable,* again and again. The repetitions, while suggesting his limitations, serve to reinforce the novel's themes and Huck's preoccupations. In the same way, Huck has certain pet phrases like *pretty soon* and *by and by* that seemingly signify little more than his imprecision about time, but reveal both the tempo of Huck's life and the importance he attaches to events.

Huck has to make each word count, and a good word often occurs with more than one meaning. For instance, Huck uses *pow-wow* once meaning "to talk" ("we would go to the cave and pow-wow over what we had done"), another time with the sense of "a great deal" ("a pow-wow of cussing"), and finally as "engine" or "engine noise" ("her lights would wink out and her pow-wow shut off"). Each of these uses is both colloquial and peculiarly American.

A brief look at any dictionary of Americanisms reveals how many first uses are credited to Twain. In Huck, Twain discovered the perfect spokesperson for the innovativeness of American English. Huck takes full advantage of English's flexibility in word function; he is particularly adept at creating finite verbs from words with a wide variety of other primary functions. When the King and the Duke first latch on to Huck and Jim, to satisfy the King's need for attention – his need to be addressed as "Your Majesty" – Huck and Jim "set to *majestying* him" (HF, Chap. 19). In the same sequence, the King sighs over his fate, and the Duke demands to know " 'What are you a*lassin'* about?' " Huck can also find new meanings for nouns and turn verbs into nouns. Having pretended at one point to choke on a chicken bone in order to stall for time, he hits another snag, "so I played another chicken-bone and got another *think*" (HF, Chap 26). Although Huck is sparing with his adjectives, when he needs a new descriptive term, he finds it. So, for example, a circus lady's dress is "rose-leafy."

The poetic qualities of the Huck Finn style are in many ways inextricably linked to its colloquialness. As Perry Miller observed, Twain "ultimately employed simplicity of style for fecundity of effect."[19] Certainly Huck's constant lexical resourcefulness constitutes poetic creativity. But over and above the tremendous inventiveness of Huck's vocabulary and the authenticity of the dialect forms stands Twain's skillful use of alliteration and verbal imagery of all sorts, particularly hyperbole, metaphor, and onomatopoeia.

In the sunrise passage, for example, Huck's poetic constructions are simple and down-to-earth, reflecting his own experience. He has certainly heard "bull frogs a-cluttering" (onomatopoeia). His frequent night excursions would make him familiar with quiet "like the whole world was asleep" (simile),[20] and his affinity with nature makes his description of "everything smiling in the sun" (personification) totally appropriate. Furthermore, Huck's understanding of nature leads him to present his perceptions as concrete qualities of the external world. Thus, he sees the river "soften up" and change color from black to gray. Alliteration in the sunrise passage centers on the silibant /s/, which suggests the hushed calm pervading the scene – *streaks/sometimes/sweep/screaking/still/sounds/see/ streak/snag/swift/sweet/smell/smiling/sun/song-birds*. Many of Huck's descriptions are rich in sense imagery. Charles Clerc notes that, using traditional classifications, Twain manages to get four of the five senses into the sunrise scene – sight, smell, touch, and sound.[21]

In his description of the thunderstorm on Jackson's Island, Huck uses an onomatopoetic word – *fst* – for a syntatic transition ("and next, when it was just about the bluest and blackest – *fst!* it was as bright as glory"). Similarly, the thunder goes "rumbling, grumbling, tumbling, down the sky towards the under side of the world." Finally, Huck uses a homely simile to liken the sound to "rolling empty barrels down stairs, – where it's long stairs and they bounce a good deal, you know."

Despite his extraordinary verbal facility and inventiveness, Huck is a most unassuming narrator. His style is so colloquial and seemingly unaffected and unrehearsed that we frequently feel as if he is carrying on a conversation with us. This effect is heightened by his liberal use of direct addresses to "you," the reader. When Huck describes his own activity or an event in nature, Twain seems most able to balance his art with the artlessness of Huck's voice. When Huck accounts for what he hears, reads, or observes in social settings, his narrative voice, while no less entertaining, seems somewhat more contrived. As Henry Nash Smith notes, although Huck is "primarily an observer," he "is endowed with Mark Twain's own unambiguous attitude toward the fraud and folly he witnesses."[22]

One contrivance that most readers happily overlook with the appropriate "suspension of disbelief" is Huck's ability to remember and report verbatim lengthy direct accounts of other characters' speech and writing. In fact, among these reports are some of the novel's most amusing sections. Our delight in Emmeline Grangerford's doggerel "Ode to Stephen Dowling Bots" and in the Duke's shameless distortion of Hamlet's soliloquy is heightened by Huck's sober admiration. These fabrications are pure Twain; Huck serves as an excuse to create them. They have little to do with Huck's story except insofar as they capture the essence of what passed for culture in rural pre–Civil War America. Of course, they also serve as additional proof of Huck's naiveté and in that way further endear him to the reader.

A few of these social commentaries are meant to instruct rather than amuse. One such passage is the "half-a-man" speech that Colonel Sherburn addresses to the lynch mob headed by Buck Harkness. Smith comments that "the Sherburn episode seems unusually isolated. None of the principal characters is involved in or affected by it . . . and Huck is a spectator whom even the author hardly notices" (p. 135). By comparison, Pap's rather lengthy diatribe against the "govment" seems to belong in the novel and in Huck's memory. It develops Pap's character as town drunk, petty philosopher, and racist, and it is likely that Huck has heard some version of the speech on many occasions: "Whenever his liquor begun to work, he most always went for the govment" (Chap. 6).

Twain carefully differentiates the style in these "speeches" to represent the speakers. His prefatorial note to *Huckleberry Finn* speaks eloquently for his attention to his characters' voices:

> In this book a number of dialects are used, to wit: the Missouri negro dialect; the extremest form of the backwoods South-Western dialect; the ordinary "Pike-County" dialect; and four modified vari-

eties of this last. The shadings have not been done in a hap-hazard fashion, or by guess-work; but pains-takingly, and with the trustworthy guidance and support of personal familiarity with these several forms of speech.

Although Twain had a very good ear, he uses dialect variations principally for characterization and only secondarily for linguistic authenticity.[23]

For example, Pap and Colonel Sherburn have many rhetorical devices in common. They pose questions and offer the answers — " 'And what do you reckon they said? Why, they said . . . ' "; " 'Do I know you? I know you clear through' " (HF, Chaps. 6 and 22). They repeat key words, uttering them in apparent disgust. But Pap's speech represents the ramblings of a drunk. He is contemptible and even occasionally amusing, for example, when he describes his broken-down old hat. He sounds like Huck. He uses the "a-" participles — "a-standing" and "a-coming." He uses multiple negatives, incorrectly formed superlatives ("awfulest"), contractions, parentheticals, and many *ands* to link ideas.

Although the colonel's language shares some of these features ("pitifulest"), it is in general both more sophisticated and more standard. Most readers will not condone Sherburn's lawlessness or his arrogance, but he does not seem contemptible or in the least amusing. Pap is certainly as dangerous as the colonel, but the colonel's language requires him to be taken more seriously.

Huck recounts many dialogues in the course of telling his story. Dialogues move the story along, providing both drama and moments when the action can pause. But an important purpose of most dialogues is to let characters speak for themselves. Readers have an opportunity to view characters from different angles as they hear them interacting with one another. In a first-person narrative, dialogues allow the narrator to portray himself in different ways and to comment on other characters with his introductions and transitions or "stage directions," as Twain called the tags introducing and following directly reported discourse.[24]

One of the best-constructed dialogues in the novel is a conversation between the Duke and the King after their Wilks scam collapses and they have escaped the town and returned to the raft. The gold that they stole and Huck hid in Wilks's coffin excites so much interest when it is discovered that the scoundrels are able to flee, but neither of them knows how the gold got there. Huck is, of course, a silent party to their conversations; his fate rests on how they resolve the issue.

Throughout the interchange, heavy with pregnant pauses, the reader shares Huck's tension about the outcome. Huck's tags, "kind of absent-minded like," "kinder slow, and deliberate, and sarcastic," "kind of ruffles up," "pretty brisk," "bristles right up" (HF, Chap. 30) involve careful observation combined with understatement to catch the nuances of sarcasm, indignation, and anger as the two participants become increasingly frustrated with one another.

As the Duke and the King spar back and forth, their language is a perfect reflection of their approaches to life. The King is lazy, insinuating, and somewhat sniveling; the Duke is sarcastic, aggressive, and quick. As in any ordinary conversation, the two play off each other's words; when the King leads off with " 'Mf! And we reckoned the *niggers* stole it,' " the Duke counters with " 'Yes . . . we did.' " Then they bounce it back and forth: " 'Leastways — I did' "; " 'On the contrary — I did.' " When the Duke says " 'Don't you reckon I know who hid the money in that coffin?' " The King shouts back, " '*Yes*, sir! I know you *do* know. . . .' "

In the course of this interchange, the King manages to become genuinely confused, and although he confesses because the Duke physically abuses him, he is left with questions. The Duke is unshakable in his convictions, refusing even to acknowledge the fact that it was his idea to add their money to Peter Wilks's — to make up "the deffersit" between what Wilks actually left and what he said he left. The Duke gets in the last word: " 'G'long to bed — and don't you deffersit *me* no more deffersits, long's *you* live!' " For these two con men, who live by their wits and their tongues, the glibbest is also the strongest.

Many of the dialogues in the novel involve Huck interacting with strangers he encounters. In almost every instance, he is wary and cautious in these exchanges, frequently spinning lies to cover up his true purpose and identity. He relies upon the fact that people are frequently lonely, like to hear themselves talk, and are starved for some excitement. In his conversation early in the novel with Mrs. Judith Loftus, with just a little prompting she tells him everything he wants to know about town gossip surrounding Jim's and his disappearances. Although she sees through his masquerade as a girl, she also provides him with an explanation: " 'You've been treated bad, and you made up your mind to cut. Bless you, child, I wouldn't tell on you!' " (HF, Chap. 11).

In a parallel conversation toward the end of the novel, Huck arrives at the Phelps farm, trusting to Providence to help him find a way to free Jim. Without uttering more than half a dozen words, Huck passes himself off as cousin Tom, learns he's with Aunt Sally, and explains his presence by agreeing with Aunt Sally that his boat had, in fact, gone aground.

Huck's reticence not only allows him to gather information, it plants ideas in other people's minds. He convinces slave hunters, who approach the raft, that his family is down with smallpox by asking for help but refusing to explain why he needs it.

> "It's the-a-the-well, it ain't anything much."
> They stopped pulling. It warn't but a mighty little way to the raft, now. One says:
> "Boy, that's a lie. What *is* the matter with your pap? Answer up square now, and it'll be the better for you."
> "I will, sir, I will, honest — but don't leave us, please. It's the — the — gentlemen, if you'll only pull ahead, and let me heave you the head-line, you won't have to come a-near the raft — please do."
> (HF, Chap. 16).

In terms of sheer linguistic ingenuity, probably no other dialogue in the novel can match the one between the "brothers" and the "sisters" on the Phelps farm after Huck and Tom help Jim escape. Each of the country people tries to outdo the other in recounting the outlandish details of Jim's escape. Their spirited talk is punctuated by explanations and interruptions, as well as little asides — " 'pass that air sasser o' m'lasses, won't ye' " (HF, Chap. 41). Finally, Aunt Sally gets in the last word as she recounts in detail the aggravation and fear she experienced as a result of the events of the preceding days.

Twain expended real care on these exchanges. These people share many dialect features with Huck and Pap, and their talk is liberally sprinkled with dialect pronunciations — "that-air," "sich," "fust," "kivered" – and some eye dialect – "wuz," "cretur."[25] But it is the idiosyncrasies of the individual speakers that really makes the passage work. Mrs. Hotchkiss is fond of quoting herself; "s'I" is a running refrain, played off in one case against "s'e" for "says he" and in another against "sh-she" for "says she." She leads off the "clacking" and picks up whenever another speaker stops to breathe – " 'My very *words,* Brer Penrod' "; " 'You may *well* say it, Brer Hightower!' " When Sister Phelps pauses dramatically in the middle of her account – " 'You explain *that* to me, if you can! – *any* of you!' " – she is met with an appreciative chorus of support:

"Well, it does beat – "
"Laws alive, I never –"
"So help me, I wouldn't a be – "
"*House* thieves as well as – "
"Goodnessgracioussakes, I'd a ben afeard to *live* in sich a – "

Huck offers no commentary on this dialogue. He is preoccupied with the dangers facing Jim and Tom, and he is an outsider in this setting. The dialogue provides dramatic evidence of the degree to which Tom's childish desire for adventure has worked up the country folks, thereby creating even greater dangers for Jim. It also attests to Huck's lack of control in the last section of the novel.

The relationship that develops between Huck and Jim provides, for many readers, the most lasting memory of the novel. Ironically, the antiestablishment, antireligious stance Huck must assume to befriend Jim and Twain's characterization of Jim are also the novel's most controversial aspects. Banned on occasion for the former, the novel has been removed from reading lists more recently for the latter. Some modern audiences have found that the portrait of Jim, however it grows and changes in the novel, is still stereotyped and demeaning to blacks. To be sure, Twain had a southerner's ambivalence about blacks. On the one hand, he expressed both respect and affection; on the other hand, he could condescend and patronize. Some of this ambivalence certainly comes through in his portrayal of Jim.

Twain was among a handful of white writers who explored seriously the complexities of race relations and invested black characters with dignity and power. In "A True Story," a short story that he wrote for the *Atlantic Monthly* in 1874, he has an ex-slave, Aunt Rachel, describe separation from and ultimate reunion with her son. The narrative technique in this story involved a considerable advance for him in using both a first-person and a vernacular narrator in a totally serious and unfiltered presentation.

Prior to writing this story, Twain had used the vernacular primarily for humorous storytelling. However, as Tony Tanner notes, "in this story the accents of the outlaw reveal a new dimension of moral potential, a new ability to articulate serious human emotions."[26] The societal outcast, an ex-slave, teaches a lesson of deep suffering and strength to her supposed superior, the naive young man who introduces her tale. Twain added immeasurably to the power and dignity of the story by having Aunt Rachel tell it in what seem to the reader to be her own words, without the interruption of a more sophisticated narrator.

In creating Jim's character and speech in *Huckleberry Finn,* Twain was certainly mindful of the fact that he was already stretching the limits of public tolerance with Huck's narration. Although Jim is multidimensional and complex, Twain maintained a clear division between the white and black characters. Moreover, he distinguished consistently between their speech. Twain was an astute enough observer of dialect variation to recognize many of the features of vernacular black English long before linguists began detailed dialect studies.

From the moment Jim appears, he represents Twain's "Missouri negro dialect." When he says " 'Who dah?' " he doesn't use the copula; he substitutes initial *d* for initial *th;* and he drops his final - *r.* The first and second features are typical of black English, although the second occurs in other dialects as well; the third is typical of southern American English. When Jim says " 'Say — who is you? Whar is you? Dog my cats if I didn't hear sumf'n. Well, I knows what I's gwyne to do. I's gwyne to set down here and listen tell I hears it agin' " (HF, Chap. 2) — the third-person *is, knows,* and *hears* with *I* and *you* is common in black English, as is the *f* for medial *th* in "sumf'n." The other dialect features are typically nonstandard, but Twain uses more elaborate dialect spelling for Jim. White characters say "goin"; Jim and other black characters say "gwyne."

Jim as a character changes in the course of the novel. As a slave he seems simple and childlike, but as an independent partner with Huck in their river trip, his superstitions become useful insights and his feelings and thoughts become more profound. As Huck's respect for Jim grows, so does Jim's character. His language, however, is generally consistent. In his most memorable speeches, he is both articulate and powerful. The difference between his speech and Huck's rests on a few dialect features and spellings rather than on word choice or syntax.

One of the novel's finest speeches, and surely one of the most poignant in American literature, is Jim's mournful account to Huck of how he discovered that his four-year-old daughter Elizabeth had lost her hearing from a bout of scarlet fever. He had ordered her to shut a door and when she didn't obey, he hit her, but her only reaction was to cry.

> "My, but I *wuz* mad, I was agwyne for de chile, but jis' den – it was a do' dat open innerds – jis' den, 'long come de wind en slam it to, behine de chile, ker-*blam!* – en my lan', de chile never move'! My breff mos' hop outer me, en I feel so-so – I doan' know *how* I feel. I crope out, all a-tremblin', en crope aroun' en open de do' easy en slow, en poke my head in behine de chile, sof' en still, en all uv a sudden, I says *pow!* jis' as loud as I could yell. *She never budge!"* (HF, Chap. 24)

With the exception of one word, *wind,* Twain consistently represents the black English feature of consonant cluster reduction, in which the second of two consonants in final word position is lost – *'chile, jis', behine, move', lan', en,* and so on. He also uses the initial *d* for *th* and the final *f* for *th.* Jim's language looks more nonstandard because of the eye dialect Twain employs – *wuz, uv.* However, aside from the dialect and a few idiosyncratic forms – *my, my lan* – this could be Huck talking. The parenthetical aside – "it was a do' dat open innerds"; the onomatopoeia – "ker-*blam*"; the balanced modification – "easy en slow," "sof' en still"; and the syntactic arrangement of active verbs linked with *and* – "en crope aroun' en open de do' . . . en poke my head in" are all very similar to Huck's style.

No matter how eloquent Jim is, the special dialect forms that distinguish his speech create a barrier for the reader. But when Huck reports what Jim says, that barrier is removed. In the climactic passage of the novel, Huck's memory of Jim's voice and his report of Jim's words prompt him to tear up his letter to Miss Watson turning Jim in and to decide to rescue Jim and "go to hell." Huck's memories of his "adventures" center on his relationship with Jim on the river. He sees and hears Jim:

> . . . and I see Jim before me, all the time, in the day, and in the night-time, sometimes moonlight, sometimes storms, and we a floating along, talking, and singing, and laughing. But somehow I couldn't seem to strike no places to harden me against him, but only the other kind. I'd see him standing my watch on top of his'n, stead of calling me – so I could go on sleeping; and see him how glad he was when I come back out of the fog; and when I come to him again in the swamp, up there where the feud was; and such-like times; and would always call me honey, and pet me, and do everything he could think of for me, and how good he always was; and at last I struck the time I saved him by telling the men we had small-pox aboard, and he was so grateful, and said I was the best friend old Jim ever had in the world, and the *only* one he's got now; and then I happened to look around, and see that paper. (HF, Chap. 31)

When Huck says of Jim, "and said I was the best friend old Jim ever had in the world, and the *only* one he's got now," the present-tense verb ("he's got") and the *now* suggest that Huck is interpreting his relationship to Jim at the moment he is making his decision. However, the phrase seems to be embedded in what Jim said about events earlier in the novel. In fact, Huck is repeating almost verbatim Jim's earlier speech in Chapter 16; " 'you's de bes' fren' Jim's ever had; en you's de *only* fren' ole Jim's got now.' "

When Jim says it, it sounds like pleading, not an affirmation of a friendship between equals. When Huck remembers it, Jim's fate still rests in his hands, but the memory captures Huck's commitment as well as Jim's. Jim is not present to make his case in person; it is Huck's memory of Jim and Jim's words that determines his change of heart. As James M. Cox notes, "Huck has internalized the image of Jim."[27] Huck and Jim's voice have become one.

In *Huckleberry Finn* Twain discovered a unique combination of character, narrator, and subject matter that allowed him to concentrate his effort on developing the colloquial style into a powerfully poetic medium. In this passage, all of those pieces come together. There is no pretense, no particular drama to be played out, not even a specific moment or scene to be recorded. It is pure Huck. The language captures Huck's memories of the happiest moments he shared with Jim on the river. The river's gentle motion comes through in the present participles and in the parallel modifiers. Huck's images of Jim rehearse the trip. What Huck "sees" are not the details of Jim's actual appearance, but Jim's kindness and the warm bond the two share.

The delicate balance that Twain maintained by using a colloquial form of English for literary purposes in *Huckleberry Finn* was not immediately clear to his contemporaries, nor was it easy for those who recognized its brilliance to imitate.[28] Twain himself never again used Huck's innovative voice effectively. Thus, for example, in *Tom Sawyer Abroad* (1894) and *Tom Sawyer, Detective* (1896), Huck narrates but Tom is the center of attention. Other narrators, Hank Morgan, for instance, in *A Connecticut Yankee in King Arthur's Court* (1889), did not limit Twain enough. Only in the "Autobiography," where he was not compelled to maintain a consistent narrative persona, does he approximate his achievement in *Huckleberry Finn*, but there his purpose was so loose that it provided no focus for the style.

Yet many of the most prominent artists of the twentieth century, including Sherwood Anderson, Hemingway, and Faulkner, have acknowledged the inspiration they derived from this novel. In *Huckleberry Finn* Twain proved the potential of the colloquial style. His challenge to traditional forms of literary discourse is one of the novel's lasting legacies to American literature.

NOTES

1 Jonathan Yardley, "Thanks, Huck Finn," *Washington (D.C.) Post*, May 7, 1984. p. C1.
2 Ibid., p. C10.
3 Albert Stone, *The Innocent Eye: Childhood in Mark Twain's Imagination* (1961; reprint New York: Archon Books, 1970), pp. 141–2.
4 Tony Tanner, *The Reign of Wonder: Naivety and Reality in American Literature* (1965; reprint New York: Harper & Row, Perennial Library, 1967), p. 105.

5 In a selection in *Mark Twain in Eruption,* ed. Bernard DeVoto (1940; reprint New York: Capricorn Books, 1968), p. 224, Twain remarks on the storyteller's art: "I mean those studied fictions which seem to be the impulse of the moment and which are so effective: such as, for instance, fictitious hesitancies for the right word, fictitious unconscious pauses, fictitious unconscious side remarks, fictitious unconscious embarrassments, fictitious unconscious emphases placed upon the wrong word with a deep intention back of it – these and all the other artful fictive shades which give to a recited tale the captivating naturalness of an impromptu narration." These devices are precisely the ones that Twain tried to transfer to the written medium in order to make Huck's speech appear unstudied and spontaneous.

6 Louis J. Budd, *Our Mark Twain: The Making of His Public Personality* (Philadelphia: University of Pennsylvania Press, 1983), p. 57.

7 Samuel Langhorne Clemens, *Mark Twain's Letters,* ed. Albert Bigelow Paine (New York: Harper & Row, 1917) vol. I, p. 227.

8 Clemens, *Letters,* vol. II, p. 797.

9 Ibid., pp. 504–5.

10 Henry Nash Smith, *Mark Twain: The Development of a Writer* (1962; reprint New York: Atheneum, 1967), p. 4.

11 Samuel Langhorne Clemens, "A Complaint about Correspondents," in *The Celebrated Jumping Frog of Calaveras County and Other Sketches* (1867; reprint Upper Saddle River, N.J.: Literature House, 1969), p. 31.

12 A term developed by Dorrit Cohn, *Transparent Minds: Narrative Modes for Presenting Consciousness in Fiction* (Princeton, N.J.: Princeton University Press, 1978), p. 190.

13 Martin Joos, *The English Verb: Form & Meanings* (Madison: University of Wisconsin Press, 1968), p. 131.

14 Cohn, *Transparent Minds,* p. 190.

15 Robert Lowenherz, "The Beginning of 'Huckleberry Finn,'" *American Speech* 38 (October 1963) 196–201.

16 Sydney J. Krause, "Twain's Method and Theory of Composition," *Modern Philology* 56 (February 1959):167–77.

17 Richard Bridgman, *The Colloquial Style in America* (New York: Oxford University Press, 1968), p. 122.

18 Chap. 25. For a more detailed analysis of this passage, see Janet Holmgren McKay, "'Tears and Flapdoodle': Point of View and Style in *The Adventures of Huckleberry Finn,*" *Style* 10 (Winter 1976):41–50.

19 Perry Miller, *Nature's Nation* (Cambridge, Mass.: Harvard University Press, 1967), p. 229.

20 When Huck and Jim pass St. Louis, Huck notes that "There warn't a sound there; everybody was asleep" (Chap. 12).

21 Charles Clerc, "Sunrise on the River: 'The Whole World' of Huckleberry Finn," *Modern Fiction Studies* 14 (Spring 1968):67–78.

22 Smith, *Mark Twain*, p. 119.

23 For a detailed study of the literary dialects in *Huckleberry Finn*, see David Carkeet, "The Dialects in *Huckleberry Finn*," *American Literature* 51 (November 1979):315–32.

24 Samuel Langhorne Clemens, "William Dean Howells," in *Howells: A Century of Criticism*, ed. Kenneth E. Eble (Dallas: Southern Methodist University Press, 1962), pp. 78–87.

25 Eye dialect refers to the practice of spelling words to look like they are normally pronounced, with no real dialect variation signified, for example, *wuz* for *was*. Some eye dialect in *Huckleberry Finn* appears to have the special purpose of identifying Huck's unfamiliarity with a term, for example, *sivilize*.

26 Tanner, *Reign of Wonder*, p. 135.

27 James M. Cox, *Mark Twain: The Fate of Humor* (Princeton, N.J.: Princeton University Press, 1966), p. 181.

28 See Bridgman, *The Colloquial Style in America*, "Copies and Misfires," pp. 131–64.

4

"Nobody but Our Gang Warn't Around": The Authority of Language in *Huckleberry Finn*

LEE CLARK MITCHELL

TOM Sawyer notoriously usurps the plot in *Adventures of Huckleberry Finn* and impairs the novel's moral structure by setting a "free nigger free." Or so many readers have claimed. The reenslavement for sheer *adventure* of a man Tom knows is legally free seems on the face of it merely grotesque; and Huck's bewildered assistance only diminishes his earlier triumphant decision to "go to hell" on behalf of Jim. Moreover, as Laurence B. Holland cogently argues, the timing of Miss Watson's manumitting will a full month before Huck's bout with conscience grants a merely "ritual" status to the scene and a tone of "futility" to the conclusion.[1]

Our discomfort, however, results less from a betrayal of Huck's decision, or even from its suppressed irrelevance, than from the lurking suspicion that his decision and the ending do not differ all that much. While we cringe at Tom's "Evasion" scheme for its deliberate and gratuitous cruelty, we cringe even more as we realize how starkly it enacts questionable terms in Huck's famous gesture. After all, Tom does no more than exploit to the fullest the principle behind Huck's reliance on "right" feeling – a principle that justifies behavior as well for nearly everyone else in the novel. Far from forming an "Evasion" of the ethical model that Huck supposedly represents, the concluding "raft of trouble" drifts to the limits of the novel's problematic implications for conduct. Even more radically, the ending confirms how dependent upon language are feelings themselves, and suggests in the process that the authority of words dictates far more than the shape of particular events. Discursive conventions actively structure the terms of personal identity in the novel – a novel that, as much as anything, is about the authoring of a self. Through the course of his narrative, Huck will create himself no less willfully than anyone else, and will do so in ways that come to seem no more self-justifiable.

The sequence of the following essay, from morality to identity to language, charts a progression among Huck's most cherished certainties about what it is possible to assume. Each one of these categories seems to him somehow more "natural" than the one preceding, and he confidently believes each stands more or less independent of the other two. Yet his narrative itself reveals language and identity (no less than morality) as social conventions, whose arbitrary and interdependent status is fully exposed only at the Phelps farm. Contrary to what most readers have suspected, then, Tom's "Evasion" appropriately concludes the novel, in terms of both formal coherence and moral obscurity. This clear thematic appropriateness notwithstanding, Tom invariably has seemed less scrupulous than Huck. And it is that falsely invidious distinction we must address first, since it results from a narrative strategy that disguises the novel's troubling resistance to fixed categories, whether moral, psychological, or linguistic.

1

That strategy begins in the boyish innocence that allows a river-rat to describe manners and mores with comic incomprehension. When Huck remarks on Miss Watson's prayerful "grumble" over food, or wonders at an undertaker's "softy soothering ways," or admires Emmeline Grangerford's lugubrious "style," the social construction of reality tumbles into view. Sometimes ridiculous, otherwise cruel conventions of behavior emerge *as* mere conventions, the more compellingly as Huck remains steadfastly oblivious to the very possibility that they are arbitrary, not natural. Yet everyone else is likewise oblivious. Miss Watson, for example, never doubts a biblical exegesis that leads her to pray in the closet, while with firmly clenched guns the Grangerfords and Shepherdsons admire a sermon on brotherly love. In obedience to the dictates of a "gentleman's" code, Colonel Sherburn will shoot a drunken Boggs. From Huck's perspective, social convention is nearly always unpredictable, violating life and sense with equal ease. Everywhere and at every level of seriousness, people justify behavior by assuming its naturalness; and because things turn out as expected, they assume their categories must be right. Only Huck's solemnly wondering gaze exposes the choplogic of such categorical imperatives.

Of course, Huck cannot question even circular reasoning, since he has yet to learn the power of intellectual abstraction. But as a child, he can impulsively reject the more brutal dictates of social convention, and he does define with Jim an apparent alternative to the self-centered, self-authorizing pattern of southern society. Their idylically drifting hours together teach Huck a goal that should justify action – one best expressed after the squabbling King and Duke first rock the raft, only to make up: "Jim and me was pretty glad to see it. It took away all the uncomfortableness, and we felt mighty good over it, because it would a been a miserable business to have any unfriendliness on the raft; for what you want, above all things, on a raft, is for everybody to be satisfied, and feel right and kind towards the others." Huck accommodates the two men to preserve the peace, not naively or out of misplaced respect. He sees through their fraudulent claims, unlike Jim, but nonetheless defers for the general welfare.

However attractive at first glance, this conjunction of Christian charity with Rousseauistic natural virtue is deeply troubling – far more so, in fact, than its quietism suggests. The problem is a logical one, and results from an inherent conflict between concepts Huck unwittingly elides in his concern to "feel right." The phrase collapses together antithetical categories by implying that emotion can legislate a standard of reason, that ethical issues can be measured affectively. Yet no external vantage point is left when morality depends so exclusively upon the authority of the self, and ethics therefore is reduced to a series of circular considerations. Huck's justification of riverside thefts, for example – "We warn't feeling just right, before that, but it was all comfortable now" – wryly masks a logic as self-confirming as that expressed by the Duke and the King, by Pap, indeed by the shore world in general. From the beginning, Huck's good "feelings" translate into considerations that can too easily be self-serving, whether of the physical comfort in smoking, eating, and wearing old clothes, or the "thrift" in refusing to spend money for the circus – "there ain't no use in *wasting* it on them." A gentle humor appears to redeem his excuses, but he transgresses convention and breaks the law out of criteria as self-reflexive as everyone else's.

That Huck at times act self-servingly or immorally is hardly consequential, however. For the crucial point is that feeling itself – any feeling whatever – cannot serve to justify. Ethics and emotion should not be confused, since the terms by which we make sense of the one differ radically from the criteria for the other. And yet Huck consistently confuses them. Take, for example, the defrauding of the Wilks girls: His emotional barometer registers first "ornery and low down and mean," then "ruther blue," and finally "dreadful glad," once he has recovered the money. While these sympathetic responses prompt him to actions that we interpret favorably, we do so despite the fact that ethical considerations are masked by the emotional drama itself. Huck laudably helps the Wilks girls because they are kind, although their kindness to him has no logical bearing on their claim to the money. The feelings that lead him to assist, in other words, are irrelevant to the girls' legal rights.

Irrelevant as emotion is to ethics, Huck nonetheless repeatedly confuses the two. Earlier, for instance, in a playful mood, he convinces Jim that a real fog was merely a dream, only then to learn that trust and good faith give greater pleasure than teasing lies. The premise again disguised by the scene, however, is that affective standards, not logical ones, have become the measure of moral conduct.[2] Huck, of course, cannot be expected to know this, since the narrative requires a childish sensibility ever ignorant of moral abstractions. Yet that strategy itself has a disturbing effect. For by celebrating an inability to distinguish the personal from the social – his own desire from collective right – the novel reduces Huck's behavior to the same self-confirming logic as everyone else's. Morally commendable as he may seem, the novel provides no terms by which that status can be confirmed. And in the end, the "right feelings" of a "sound heart" seem as arbitrary and capricious as the cruel conventions of town.

Most severely testing the category of "feeling right" are Huck's three encounters with a troubled conscience. The first, dismissively brief scene reveals only his fear of ignominy: Even though "people would call me a low down Ablitionist and despise me," he promises to keep Jim's escape a secret. In Chapter 16, when friendship conflicts with the bad "conscience" that had prompted him to inform on Jim, Huck predictably opts for "whichever come handiest." And given an emotional economy in which "the wages is just the same," he vows to go on doing so. Here as elsewhere, the narrative strategy precludes the questions implicit in that vow: How will he determine his desire? What constitutes a "sound heart?" Why prefer one action over another given contradictory feelings of equal weight?

Huck's third bout with conscience only compounds these questions and further exacerbates the issue. Having considered writing North to save Jim, he rejects the idea for three reasons: Miss Watson might resent her slave's ingratitude; Jim would be universally despised; and, most importantly (in a reversion to the first scene's rationale), "it would get all around, that Huck Finn helped a nigger to get his freedom." He therefore attempts to escape his "wicked and low-down and ornery" feeling by trying to "pray a lie." The impulse might seem an improbable one, given his professed theological skepticism, but here most dramatically the novel shows that feelings are not logical. Nor are they appropriate, as he finds when his effort all too predictably fails, a failure that in turn prompts him to prepare for prayer by the ploy of drafting an experimental letter. The letter's curious effect is to leave Huck feeling "light as a feather" – curious, because the letter itself is responsible for eliciting a condition of grace, instead of forming merely the preliminary to a prayerful state: "I felt good and all washed clean of sin for the first time I had ever felt so in my life." The narrative has again conflated categories, masking the fact that Huck never intended to mail the letter that has left him "all washed clean of sin." He gains absolution, as it were, despite a contrition that is only partial. Still, the result is that Huck recalls Jim's loving-kindness, and in the "close place" dividing conscience from heart, decides to rip up the letter and "go to hell."

This crucial scene dramatizes as nowhere else the problematic aspects of Huck's behavior, by exposing the novel's radical equation of emotion, morality, and language. Quite simply, Huck's "decision" rests on nothing more than feeling. The "conscience" of a slave-holding South, however evil, represents at least a coherent social system, just as the Grangerford–Shepherdson feud illustrates a system of prescriptive rules, however vicious. Not so Huck's seemingly humane alternative, which lacks either system or logic that might link "feeling" to something outside the self. Social conventions alone allow behavior to be both anticipated and justified, and only by organizing raw feeling into a set of predictive categories can conduct then be measured. Lacking any terms other than the narrowly personal, Huck can judge action by nothing but his own pulse. That pulse may indicate a "sound heart" on the one hand, and beat calmly to what we sense as "right feelings" on the other, but the metaphor itself reveals a morality far more circular than the conventional ethos of "conscience." Even more troubling from a larger perspective are the lack of constraints on the self. For when feeling dictates value rather than the other way around, an unmoored self risks being battered by its own inconsistent energies. This may explain why the "awful" words of Huck's supposed moral triumph seem to emerge independently, as if unintended: " . . . but they was said. And I let them stay said." Conversely, when southern values earlier impelled him to identify Jim, "the words wouldn't come" – an experience repeated when he tries to "pray a lie." Unable to structure emotion through langage, Huck finds that language at times opposes "conscience," at other times expresses it.

2

But Huck's inability to tie morality to language does not result simply from his dependence on feeling. Language in the novel more generally seems free-floating, especially as a form of self-definition. People everywhere adapt selves and adopt identities all by mere assertion: A con man becomes the late Dauphin, then in turn a pirate, Edmund Kean the Elder, the Reverend Elexander Blodgett, and Harvey Wilks; Jim becomes a "sick Arab" just as Tom becomes Sid; and Huck becomes Sarah Williams, George Peters, and George Jaxon, then Adolphus the valet, and finally Tom. Aunt Polly alone relies on ocular proof, sternly claiming to know Tom "when I *see* him"; yet her metonymic appearance as a mere pair of spectacles suggests that her logic persuades less than her tone. She knows Tom only by sight in a novel where trust in one's senses is unreliable at best and at worst quite dangerous. As the con men realize all too well, desire invariably mediates vision. An expectant Aunt Sally, for instance, actively creates the prospect of Tom out of Huck, who in the event can only perplexedly affirm her opening query: "It's *you* at last!—*ain't* it?" Later, she embraces the real Tom after his casual assurance that he is Sid, and continues the process of social creation – as the Wilks sisters had earlier kissed the two frauds, and likewise granted them a social authority.

Indeed, selves proliferate wherever desire emerges. Blithely inventing a series of identities, the Duke and the King gain beds, two servants, hundreds of dollars, and at least one bottle of whiskey.[3] The King talks the Duke "blind" at first, and then "warbling and warbling right along . . . he was actuly beginning to believe what he was saying, *himself.*" Yet although both only temporarily convince a town to take "empty names and facts . . . for *proofs,*" their exposure hardly gives comfort to those hoping for an assurance of "actuly" true identities. The novel provides after all not a shred of evidence proving that the real Wilks brothers "are who we say we are." Despite a full chapter of narrative suspense, they are vindicated by neither writing sample nor alleged tattoo. If "you couldn't tell them from the real kind," as Huck had earlier observed of the two frauds, the converse holds with at least equal force in a novel rarely given to evidential "proofs." " 'Here's your two sets o' heirs to old Peter Wilks,' " yells the crowd; " 'you pays your money and you takes your choice!' "

Huck, however, seems oblivious to the possibility, unaware of how readily language creates selves. Ever the naive realist, he continues to assume that words stand transparently for things, and believes in a literalism so severe that even prayer continues to mystify him – "I couldn't see no advantage about it."[4] The irony, of course, is that Huck himself appears as no more than a voice in the text. Constitutionally unable to accept the broader implications of figurative discourse, he cannot appreciate the terms of his own novel in which language everywhere shapes experience. His very

89

lies assume that words mirror reality rather than constitute the way things are; and with a scrupulous sensitivity to context, he fabricates tales only for self-survival (as when he quick-wittedly misleads Pap), or to protect others (as with Mrs. Judith Loftus, the slave-hunters, and Joanna Wilks), or to find Jim. True, he too seems at times "to believe what he was saying, *himself.*" But he is unable to recognize the ways in which "false" identities do alter his "true" self – an inability that both results from and contributes to his confidence in that self.

Even his dramatically experienced rebirths encourage no self-conscious sense of change. His resurrection on Jackson's Island, for example, follows the cabin death he stages for Pap, just as later he is reborn to Jim after returning to the raft. At the Phelps farm, the process recurs most explicitly when Aunt Sally suddenly names him Tom: "If they was joyful, it warn't nothing to what I was; for it was like being born again, I was so glad to find out who I was." Huck's three rebirths form a telling progression, from the physical through the social to the linguistic; and mired in words at last, he cleverly abets Sally in creating himself as Tom. Yet comically as he exposes here the set categories of language, the scene's humor depends on the exposure being unwitting, on Huck's being a mere victim of linguistic convention. His relief, in fact, results from discovering not who he is but whom others take him to be, since again he assumes that an unaltered self persists under an infinitely flexible mask. That romantic faith in a unique being somehow independent of behavior – of an inner self untouched by its expression – remains steadfast right through to the closing "Yours Truly."

Such confidence in an empirical self seems in part a bold front, however, masking a more general uncertainty in the novel between Huck's dual identities as character and author. Deny the latter role as he will, he finds it increasingly difficult to hide his authorship. Of course, an unhesitating narrative voice bespeaks an unquestionably unified self – one that must know its feelings precisely because the self at that moment *is* those feelings. And Huck seems no more able to deviate from his voice than language can veer from the illusion of referentiality. But the point (and the problem) is that his wonderfully immediate voice is indeed an illusion, fostered in the novel by his radical conflation of dual roles. Huck disguises the gap between past and present, between himself as actor and as recollective writer, by emphasizing a single identity as the coherent, fully self-consistent "I" of the text. As we shall see later, however, the narrative inadvertently belies his efforts, and reveals despite itself the evolution of an authorial voice.[5]

Despite the book's spoken modulations, in other words — so clearly heard we could almost assume it was recited — the most salient feature of the prose is that it is written. We think of Henry James's late novels, by contrast, as too plainly written and rewritten, although as it happens they were each dictated. The reason for this is that James's characters so often confess an inability to get things "right," doing so nonetheless with such verbal adroitness that we are ever aware of the shaping powers of language. Huck, on the other hand, deftly masks his discursive skills by never doubting that things are as he says. And again, the reason he does so is because he must seem somehow innocent of literary conventions — the very conventions to which he has been "sivilized" by writing the book. This admittedly characterizes a structure common to first-person narratives of the past; bridging the disjunction between events and their recounting, they recapture antecedent ignorance from a perspective of recollective knowledge. Pip in *Great Expectations,* say, or Ishmael in *Moby-Dick,* or Miles Coverdale in *The Blithedale Romance:* Each suppresses and alters information in the necessary process of establishing a narrative line. Yet none of these suppressions approaches that of *Huckleberry Finn,* in part because none of those novels so forthrightly represents the conflict of innocence and convention. Nor do the narrators themselves enter the recollected past so transparently as to make their authorial roles seem to disappear.

Huck's very narrative strategy, in fact, directly controverts his alleged faith in an integrated self that might stand somehow outside of society. The novel, that is, divides an acting self committed to the truth and ready to lie only for humane reasons, from an authoring self that willfully compounds those lies in order, as Tom says, merely to "make . . . talk." Of course, this only expresses in less charitable terms the conventional observation that Huck's lim-

91

ited comprehension contributes to the novel's dramatic irony: He sees bifocally, doing right by judging wrong. Yet that formulation disguises Huck's fundamental desire to disguise his narrative authority – his wish to tell his story at the same time that he denies any responsibility for doing so. He cannot express the desire forthrightly, for the expression itself would belie the claim; but the impulse sometimes betrays itself, as when he falls asleep during his own narrative. Unlike the retrospective view taken in the "go to hell" scene and sustained in his concluding "I slept the night through," these scenes effectively mask Huck's role as author standing outside the text. They allow him as passive character instead to shape temporal gaps into narrative suspense. Chapter 6 closes with him guarding his drunken Pap, for example, and then Chapter 7 begins: " 'Git up! what you 'bout!' I opened my eyes and looked around, trying to make out where I was."[6]

Yet Huck's authorial status disappears more dramatically when as character he suddenly loses his breath – a speechlessness, indeed voicelessness, that occurs in the novel with surprising regularity. Sophia Grangerford, for instance, suddenly embraces him for having acted as a go-between: "I was a good deal astonished, but when I got my breath I asked her . . ." And a few pages later, he escapes from the feuding families only to discover that "the raft was gone! My souls, but I was scared! I couldn't get my breath for most a minute."[7] The first-person immediacy of Huck's experience is intensified in these breathless moments of narrative stasis. Perhaps especially in a novel that exists to "make . . . talk," scenes that subvert speech paradoxically heighten the character's sensibility, and do so again at the expense of the author's controlling presence.

When Huck does at last catch his breath, he attempts further to confirm an authorial transparency by asserting the primacy of physical experience. Unlike Tom, who engages language as a play of signifiers, Huck at every point looks for verification to "reality." His relief that he swears on a dictionary, not a Bible, only seems to imply disrespect for the former; far from acknowledging the empty authority of words, his superstitious glance instead registers how fully he believes in their scriptural status. For him, they speak to an actual order beyond any conventional syntax or particular grammar. Fixed definitions tie words to a world that ever precedes them, and seems therefore more immediate.[8] Indeed, Huck at times authenticates the "reality" of experience by claiming that words too readily evoke painful experiences — as in the recollected horror of the Grangerford–Shepherdson feud. Elsewhere, he suggests the transparency of language by asserting that his adventures exceed descriptive powers, his own or anyone's.[9] Events always precede discourse for Huck, and language can do no more than turn us back to that prior order. By blinding us to the gap between life and history — by dissolving the distinction between an event and its recounting — he fosters an illusion that experience is everywhere fully present and unmediated.[10]

Indeed, so successful is this conflation of author with actor that a moment occurs when nobody seems to create the text — the "Notice" proscribing literary trespass: "Persons attempting to find a motive in this narrative will be prosecuted; persons attempting to find a moral in it will be banished; persons attempting to find a plot in it will be shot." Odd as the progressive denial of motive, moral, and plot may seem, it only more strikingly draws attention away from an apparent denial of authorship itself. Whimsical signature aside, neither the historical Sam Clemens nor the pseudonymous Mark Twain would have "posted" this literary property. Clemens's later description of the novel's conflict—"between a sound heart and a deformed conscience"—suggests he had little trouble with moral questions; likewise, Mark Twain's career as a popular lecturer and best-selling author depended on his inventive capacity for elaborating motives and plots. The mock ferocity of the "Notice" may not fit the kindly temperament of a child, perhaps especially one who soon wins our confidence with "I never seen anybody but lied." But it is Huck who regularly resists all categories — who indeed shuns anything "regular" itself, savoring his food "in a barrel of odds and ends" and blithely rejecting that most apodictic of sciences, mathematics. The novel opens, then, with a declaration aptly suited to the anticategorical propensities of its self-authoring main character.

The reason Huck would not have signed the "Notice" is consistent with his self-effacing authorial behavior throughout. Illiterate when the novel begins, he authors that part of his life in which he first learns to write, and in the process erases as fully as possible that coming to authorship itself.[11] The authorial tone of the opening "You don't know about me" soon disappears, absorbed in the engaging voice of Huck as character. With rare exceptions, the two do not again conjoin until the end, when his immediate desire to "light out for the Territory" silently conflicts with his regretful admission: ". . . if I'd a knowed what a trouble it was to make a book I wouldn't a tackled it and ain't agoing to no more." The conclusion, in other words, claims a momentarily expected liberation that denies what Huck had actually done – sat at his desk to draft the novel. If we overlook this contradiction, it is in part because the time scheme in which he learns to write is notably unclear. Still, the narrative does offer a few temporal markers: The shift from late summer illiteracy through winter schooling to the "June rise" of Jackson's Island, then the "warm weather" in which he pens his unsent letter, and the late-summer weeks at the Phelps farm all indicate that Huck begins the novel at least a year after the events recounted in the opening chapters. The "pretty soons" and "by-and-bys" that keep the narrative flowing impart a timeless immediacy to Huck's experience. But by blurring the calendar, they disguise the year that separates him from his book as fully as the narrative seems to exclude his retrospective consciousness.[12]

Huck's account differs in this regard from other first-person narratives by actively dismissing the possibility that the experiences of the novel have changed him at all. No one quarrels with a middle-aged Pip reporting his childhood dialogues with Estella and Miss Havisham, nor Ishmael with the innkeeper Coffin more than a year before his sinking and rescue. But precisely because *Huckleberry Finn* depends for its moral ironies on a childishly immediate perspective – that is, because the novel everywhere stresses Huck's inability to judge – it must *seem* to suppress the recollective, reflective role of Huck as narrator of events a year after he has experienced them.

This radical coalescence of Huck's divergent roles creates problems of the sort Leo Marx has noted in Colonel Sherburn's speech: "Because it is difficult to believe that Huck is reporting the entire speech verbatim, the author's point of view seems to penetrate the first-person mask."[13] The point is well taken, although too narrowly applied, since other scenes also require verbatim recollection — including Pap's "Call this a govment!" speech, Tom's technical description of heraldic decoration, the long ransom note the two boys send, and most prominently the Duke's "To be or not to be" soliloquy. With this last, Huck anticipates our skepticism by explaining, "I learned it, easy enough, while he was learning it to the king." Yet later events suggest that this explanation is contrived, especially given the King's superb powers of memory; his recollection of Tim Collins's account, for example, is solely responsible for the entire Wilks episode: ". . . the king told [the Duke] everything, just like the young fellow had said it — every last word." The fact, then, that months after the intricate soliloquy Huck still recalls it word for word suggests less a memory superior to the King's than an unusual narrative strategy — one that creates an author only to exclude him as anything other than a vehicle through which the past becomes present. Although the novel depends nominally on an older Huck's memory, the fact that he has apparently matured not at all calls the very terms of memory into question. To put the matter simply, has a narrating Huck actually remembered what happened, or inadvertently "painted it up considerable"? When Aunt Sally claims to " 'disremember,' " or admits to being " 'most putrified with astonishment,' " or when Tom suggests Jim send a " 'message to let the world know where he's captivated,' " are the malapropisms theirs or Huck's? The point is that, given the narrative strategy, we are not meant to measure the distance a recollective Huck has come from his earlier naive expectations. The narrative's comic effectiveness depends precisely on his ignorance of solecisms, his complete lack of amusement at the play of language that everywhere serves private interests.

All these efforts notwithstanding, a retrospective Huck cannot help stumbling into view. Slips of expression reveal a narrative self, and even his authorial presence is confirmed by the notoriously misspelled "sivilized" — an obviously written, not spoken error.[14] At other times, he makes larger narrative missteps, as when a few chapters after using the word confidently, he seems altogether innocent of the meaning of "sivilized": "so cramped up and sivilized, as they call it." But when later knowledge slips into a narrative recounted months after the events, Huck's dual perspective breaks apart – precisely because the self assumed by "Huck" can no longer appear unified. His self-consciously retrospective tone in fact emerges clearly at least twice: first when, like Hank Morgan, he cannot scratch an itch – "Well, I've noticed that thing plenty of times since" – and second, following Mary Jane Wilks's departure – "I hain't ever seen her since, but I reckon I've thought of her a many and a many a million times."

More confusing is Huck's revelation upon first seeing Jim on Jackson's Island, when he admits to not being "afraid of *him* telling the people where I was." For Huck does not know yet that the slave is a runaway, as his subsequent surprise makes all too clear, and therefore can have no assurance that an exuberant Jim would not bear the glad tidings back to town. Likewise, late in the narrative he describes with knowing impatience Uncle Silas's "pretty long blessing"; but earlier, he had wondered why the widow should "grumble a little over the victuals, though there warn't really anything the matter with them." This progression certainly represents a gain in knowledge from Huck's point of view as a character (he now is familiar with the social ritual of grace before meals); but from his larger authorial perspective, the inconsistency suggests mere narrative manipulation. And although manipulation of events for narrative suspense forms a basic convention of first-person accounts, manipulation of language does not.

The verbal slips that bring an authoring Huck to life reveal as well the novel's narrative law – the same expensive premise that structures Jim's story of bewitchery: " . . . every time he told it he spread it more and more." From the opening reminder ("without you have read a book") on through to Tom's concluding escapades, the novel assumes the constant expandability of stories. Huck breathes life into each of them, linking each into the circular narrative line of the novel – from the widow's account of Moses, to Jim's bewitched flight and his hairball prediction, to Tom's renditions of Scott and Cervantes, to Huck's school-prize account of George Washington, and many others. Once again, the expansive nature of these stories highlights Huck's authorial role, directing us from the narrative subject back to the narrating shaper.

The novel's structure compounds this effect by a similarly circular movement that brings us back to end where we began. In the beginning, Tom wants to tie Jim, Pap is supposedly dead, and Huck claims to have "lit out" from the Widow Douglas's "siviliz-ing"; the novel concludes with Tom having "tied" Jim, Pap finally pronounced dead, and Huck planning to "light out," this time "for the Territory." The Duke and the King enter the novel having barely escaped tarring and feathering, and leave it tarred and feathered, The whole, in other words, develops not according to the linear progression of history, but out of a repetitive, recol-lective motion that seems to abrogate time – a narrative motion best exemplified in the self-circling pattern of Tom's cruel attempt to "set a free nigger free." By repeatedly turning back on itself, just as by its narrative expansions, the novel further exposes an au-thoring Huck who does not quite succeed in disguising discourse in story. That failure, moreover, further unsettles the illusion of his youthfully immediate integrity.

3

The very self-encircling narrative within which Huck expresses his naive realism reveals instead a self created entirely through lan-guage. By contrast with the complacent narrative voice of *The Adventures of Tom Sawyer* (1876), the first-person vernacular, char-acteristic dialects, and vivid idioms of *Huckleberry Finn* deny any possibility that language might achieve transparency, or attain some privileged relation to experience. On the contrary, a universe of discourses compete in the novel almost from the opening "Ex-planation" – without which "many readers would suppose that all these characters were trying to talk alike and not succeeding." The point is not merely that human voices all clamor for narrative attention. The natural world itself teems with language – with the wind "trying to whisper something to me and I couldn't make out what it was" and squirrels that "jabbered at me very friendly." In this midwestern Babel, even silence speaks, as Huck and Jim laze around "listening to the stillness."

Everywhere the novel illustrates that the power of words does not derive from any putative hold on reality. The surfeit of lan-guage suggests on the contrary the inadequacy, indeed the unreliability, of any single voice.[15] Take Huck, for example, whose prose sometimes stymies us even as the words of others confuse him. Explaining his formal address of the King, he uses opaquely double-negative terms: " 'No, your majesty' — which was the way I always called him when nobody but our gang warn't around." Likewise, in his third bout with conscience, he chides himself ambiguously for having helped Jim: ". . . whilst I was stealing a poor old woman's nigger that hadn't ever done me no harm."[16] As the scene bears out, however, it is indeed Jim, not Miss Watson, who "hadn't ever done me no harm" and on whose behalf Huck finally decides. HIs syntax unpacks counter to intention, to reveal not merely a misuse of words but how powerfully they expose truths their users may not anticipate.

Language does this precisely because it is an arbitrary convention and not a natural order; like other symbolic systems, it reveals its users as well as their subjects. At a simpler level of convention, when Jim claims transcendentally that "signs is *signs*," he grants an immanent significance to natural experience that closely resembles Huck's honoring of social and linguistic codes.[17] Yet from its opening "Notice," the novel warns us off such codifying, and quietly suggests through the lack of narrative consequences that signs may well be *merely* signs. Nothing ensues when Huck accidentally burns a spider, topples a saltcellar, or touches a snakeskin, and even results that are predicted hardly confirm predictability. Birds in erratic flight forebode rain, as Jim's hairy chest augurs wealth; but although rain and "wealth" do finally occur, no causal relationship links sign with experience. Notwithstanding Huck's assurance that "the birds was right," the suspicion lingers that they were fortuitous. Signs is *signs*, Jim fervently claims — but since they are read into, not out of nature, from a frequently post hoc and eminently human impulse, we grant him only a tautology.

Huck's discussion with Joanna Wilks of the "dreadful pluribus-unum mumps" clarifies this inversion of language and effect, this toxic virus of sign and sequence that spreads so contagiously through the novel:

". . . what in the nation do they call it the *mumps* for?"
"Why, because it *is* the mumps. That's what it starts with."

"Well, ther' ain't no sense in it. A body might stump his toe, and
take pison, and fall down the well, and break his neck, and bust his
brains out, and somebody come along and ask what killed him, and
some numskull up and says, 'Why, he stumped his *toe*'. Would ther'
be any sense in that? *No*. And ther' ain't no sense in *this*, nuther. Is
it ketching?" (Chapter 28)

The final query proves after all that, whatever may be true of the
"dreadful pluribus-unum mumps," senselessness itself is certainly
"ketching." Huck's feverish logic, moreover, forms merely a less
virulent strain of that which breaks out wherever the King and the
Duke alight. By making explicit the Humpty-Dumpty issue of
whose meanings are to apply, those cynical wordsmiths dramatically expose the conventionality of signs, the priority of texts over
experience. " 'I say orgies,' " the King explains, " 'not because it's
the common term, because it ain't—obsequies bein' the common
term – but because orgies is the right term . . . Orgies is better,
because it means the thing you're after, more exact.' " This quint-
essentially expresses one of the novel's major conclusions: that in
a world of arbitrary codes, experience can always reduce to mere
assertion, and that profit too often flows to the masters of "hum-
bug talky-talk."

Huck himself seems to learn this when he tricks Jim into believing that a dream, not a fog, has separated them. Allowing Jim to
weave a wildly inventive narrative, he suddenly reverses himself
by pointing to "trash" – prompting Jim's angry declamation, and
in turn Huck's abashed vow to "do him no more mean tricks."
The suppressed point, however, is that in his own enthusiastic
moments, Jim has likewise compelled others into his fictions –
most signally in his early story of bewitchery. Later, imprisoned at
the Phelps farm, he joins Tom and Huck in denying what the slave
Ned has so obviously heard – much as Huck had done to Jim.
Granted that Jim, unlike Huck and Tom, actually believes his fictions. Nonetheless, the moral implications of a storyteller's intentions come to seem less important than the power of his story. The
novel, in other words, celebrates inventiveness itself, and in the
process seems to present contrary positions as equally desirable.
Huck's teasing of Jim in the "trash" scene may teach him the need
for mutual trust, but the narrative otherwise contradicts his peni-

tent mood by affirming an imaginative play that unsettles others' assurances.

The play of language has a dizzying effect upon no one so much as Huck, largely because he more than others is motivated by the oxymoronic desire to "feel right." On the way to the Phelps farm, for example, he agreeably trusts to the very "Providence" that a chapter earlier was "slapping me in the face and letting me know my wickedness." But now he reflects that "Providence always did put the right words in my mouth, if I left it alone." The contrary assertions reflect Huck's continuing uncertainty about the status of his words and therefore of his self. Not only does he confuse Providence with instinct ("I go a good deal on instinct"), but this time he will be left "up a stump," without the "right words" he needs.[18] On the other hand, when "Providence" does put words in his mouth, he feels alarmed – as when he tells Mary Jane that her slaves will be reunited: "Laws it was out before I could think! . . . I see I had spoke too sudden, and said too much."

Despite what Huck has learned from Jim on the raft, the formidable "resks" posed by sincerity and honesty continue to trouble him:

> I reckon a body that ups and tells the truth when he is in a tight place, is taking considerable many resks . . . and yet here's a case where I'm blest if it don't look to me like the truth is better, and actuly *safer*, than a lie. I must lay it by in my mind, and think it over some time or other, it's so kind of strange and unregular. I never see nothing like it. Well, I says to myself at last, I'm agoing to chance it; I'll up and tell the truth this time, though it does seem most like setting down on a kag of powder and touching it off, just to see where you'll go to. (Chapter 28)

Like the notion of a transparent language, uncontingent truth seems explosively unreliable to someone who has so often seen others shape words to ends they happen to define as true. In the ensuing conversation with Mary Jane, for example, Huck continues to speak honestly (if not quite straightforwardly). And yet language still seems self-dictating: "Saying them words put a good idea in my head." With much the same effect as it had earlier in the novel, when he races back from Mrs. Judith Loftus, language seems to be speaking through Huck. Yelling unreflectively – "Git up and hump yourself, Jim! . . . They're after us!" — he never considers that the slave-hunters are not in fact actually looking for him. After all, he is safely "dead" and no longer an object of pursuit.

Although this impulsive identification with Jim defines a praiseworthy change in Huck's character, it also points to the troublingly unstable intersection of language and the self in the novel. Huck at some times relies on an independent "truth" that as here seems to speak through him, and at other times on a verbal talent that self-protectively disguises the truth. Yet in either case, truth is less at issue than the fact that words seem beyond conscious control. Incapable of using language to separate public ethics from private impulse, unable to distinguish the abstract from the immediate, Huck can only be startled by, and sometimes even balk at, his own behavior.

The simple way to maintain composure in the sort of world that Huck describes is to acknowledge how fully language creates the self. Of course, selves created wholly in this fashion invariably reshape the structure of language — by which paradoxical standard, Tom Sawyer becomes the novel's hero. Appearing in the opening sentence as a character in another novel, his intertextual identity extends to his verbal defense: "Because it ain't in the books so, that's why." He too compels words to mean what he wants, equating ransom with murder and pickaxes with case knives, then recreating garter snakes as rattlers, huts as prisons, and stairs as lightning rods. Tom will "let on" that the proposed escape took all of thirty-seven years, and will arbitrarily deny both Ned's and Aunt Sally's assumptions that things are what they manifestly seem. In this, he differs little from Aunt Sally herself, who delights in fooling her long-suffering husband about Huck's arrival: " 'I'll play a joke on him.' " For them, as for the Duke, the King, and Huck, conventional expectation offers just the toehold imaginative play requires. And it is important to recognize that although Tom's antics may pall long before Jim complains — " 'Yes . . . but what kine er time is *Jim* havin?' " — his efforts "to set a free nigger free" serve the sole end of sheer exuberant adventure.[19] Unlike the two frauds, unlike Huck himself, Tom has in mind no practical motive.[20] Huck's naive admiration of his imaginative spirit, of Tom's willingness to treat everything as an adventure of language, contributes to the novel's ironic power; but that admiration also reflects how much Huck's narrative celebrates the kind of inventive style Tom embodies.

Although Tom's "Evasion" exceeds in cruelty anything Huck does, then, their moral (and linguistic) categories nonetheless seem in the end to differ little. Huck, no less than Tom, relies on the self-justification of "feeling right," and although his feelings are largely benign, even beneficent, they are no more legitimate than anyone else's. Indeed, his major scenes of conscience vindicate a "sound heart" only by dramatizing his inability to ground right action in anything other than feeling. Just as the ending's narrative structure resembles that of the rest of the novel, its causal and moral progressions play out the pattern everywhere implicit. The very unsavoriness of Tom's plan highlights the logical inconsistency of the terms by which Huck has been acting all along. Tom flagrantly ignores consequences, it is true, but Huck pays them little more attention, and dismisses them altogether in his major bouts with conscience. With none of the families he meets, moreover, does he need the elaborate schemes he devises. The escape plan he develops at the Wilkses', like the lies he tells the Grangerfords and the Phelpses ("they froze to me for two hours; and at last when my chin was so tired it couldn't hardly go, any more") differs in degree but not kind from Tom's plot. When Jim protests that boarding the wrecked *Walter Scott* involves too much "'resk,'" Huck retorts: "'Do you reckon Tom Sawyer would ever go by this thing? Not for pie, he wouldn't. He'd call it an adventure.'"

Indeed, the novel links language and adventure by tacitly broaching this question of "resk" – a question best defined, as it happens, in Jim's response to Solomon's supposed wisdom. He rejects the biblical judgment, failing to realize that Solomon only pretended a threat and never intended to harm the infant. Yet as Jim wisely notes, "'de *real* pint is down furder,'" for had its mother not spoken, the child might well have been destroyed.[21] No risk had existed prior to his threat, but through the action of language Solomon introduced danger, and whatever his intention, the effect is the same. Fake threats, in other words, become real by virtue of contexts (particularly royal ones) that require them to be interpreted as such. Similarly, Tom's escape plan, like Huck's narration, creates for others a series of increasing hazards. Or as Huck incisively explains in response to the doctor's query about Tom's wound: " 'He had a dream, and it shot him.' " To follow Jim's advice and " 'run no resk' " is not merely to defuse adventures, but as well in the process to void language of its power.

The problem in *Huckleberry Finn* is that it disguises the dangers it seems to reveal by leading us to believe that Tom's cruelty and Huck's kindness are motivated differently. The two boys in fact differ far less than appearances would suggest. With seeming innocence, Huck repeatedly claims to want not to act, and yet nonetheless does so as contrivedly as Tom. Listen to the way he deplores his efforts at the Wilkses:

> Now how do *I* know whether to write to Mary Jane or not? Spose she dug him up and didn't find nothing—what would she think of me? Blame it, I says, I might get hunted up and jailed; I'd better lay low and keep dark, and not write at all; the thing's awful mixed, now; trying to better it, I've worsened it a hundred times, and I wish to goodness I'd just let it alone, dad fetch the whole business! (Chapter 27)

Yet in the end, Huck controls all "pretty neat—I reckoned Tom Sawyer couldn't a done it no neater himself." He may earlier have dismissed "Tom Sawyer's lies," but on the raft, he readily plays a "sivilizing" guide to Jim's guileless incomprehension. Too much should not be read into the role that Huck accepts with belated relief – "Being Tom Sawyer was easy and comfortable" – but the identification is hardly gratuitous. For the fundamental similarities between the two boys structure a novel that maintains a consistent set of assumptions, one more troubling in its consistency than most readers have allowed.

Tom's "raft of trouble" at the Phelps farms, in other words, resembles the raft that has drifted through the rest of the novel. The ending does no more than extend and elaborate the early questioning of straightforward claims for morality and identity, and more generally, for language. Not slavery alone, but all codes and structures, are exposed as arbitrary human conventions, denying therefore the inherent validity of any institution. Early and late, the novel dismisses the notion that language represents rather than creates, just as it undermines belief in the possibility of fixed, unchanging identity. Moral categories may not collapse, but no terms appear by which to affirm or apply them, and they thereby effectively disappear. The original "Notice" wryly misleads, then, by implying that poachers might indeed find moral, motive, or plot. For these are categories that can only be imported into, not discovered in, this text. As we have seen, Huck's confused morality depends upon a confused language that allows him to be two things at once – narrator and character, passive and active, morally right yet emotionally satisfied. The book has it two ways to the very end, where Huck escapes from authority only to author his book. Like many another American text, it asserts freedom with the very arguments, in the very tones, that belie the assertion.

NOTES

1 Laurence B. Holland, "A 'Raft of Trouble': Word and Deed in *Huckleberry Finn*," in *Glyph 5* (Baltimore: The Johns Hopkins University Press, 1979), pp. 69–87. Holland stands nearly alone in accepting the ending's implications for the novel: ". . . the closing section does not wrench the book from its course; it reveals in sharper light the profound irony that governs the book." For another reading that accepts the ending on quite different terms, see James M. Cox, *Mark Twain: The Fate of Humor* (Princeton, N.J.: Princeton University Press, 1966), pp. 156–84.

2 This pattern is hardly rare in American literature, reaching back beyond Emerson's and Thoreau's reliance on the authority of the individual "conscience." Yet to take only the example of *Uncle Tom's Cabin*, it forms the major flaw in Harriet Beecher Stowe's "solution" to the problem of antebellum slavery. Her reliance on voluntary manumission offers no terms, other than "feeling right," by which to persuade others.

3 Compare Pap's similar self-created reformation, which wins him a jug of "forty-rod."

4 On only one occasion does Huck reconsider the efficacy of prayer, when loaves of bread float down the river to Jackson's Island: "So there ain't no doubt but there is something in that thing" (Chapter 8).

5 Alan Trachtenberg has nicely observed that "to be himself Huck must hide himself," and anticipates some points of my argument in pursu-

ing the question, "Who is the controlling comedian of the book, Huck or Mark Twain?" See "The Form of Freedom in *Adventures of Huckleberry Finn*," *Southern Review* 6, n.s. (Autumn 1970):954–71.

6 For other examples of such somnolent storytelling, see Chapters 7, 8, and 13.

7 Huck's loss of voice also occurs in Chapters 4, 8, 13, 29, and 30.

8 See, for instance, his lexical specifying of "towhead" (Chapter 12) or his claim: "Anybody that don't believe yet . . . will believe it now, if they read on" (Chapter 16).

9 In Chapter 7, he had complained about the inadequacy of his vocabulary: "You know what I mean–I don't know the words to put in." Later, in Chapter 29, he asserts: "the way I lit out . . . there ain't nobody can tell."

10 Richard Bridgman has analyzed the technique of Huck's "self-effacing" style in *The Colloquial Style in America* (New York: Oxford University Press, 1966), pp. 78–130. See also George C. Carrington, Jr., *The Dramatic Unity of "Huckleberry Finn"* (Columbus: Ohio State University Press, 1976), pp. 111–21.

11 Laurence B. Holland nicely qualifies this claim by identifying what he refers to as the novel's "illusion of remembering." For another discussion of the "authorial personality telling the story," see Louis D. Rubin, Jr., *The Teller in the Tale* (Seattle: University of Washington Press, 1967), pp. 42–82.

12 Barry A. Marks assumes that "the text makes clear that Huck begins his story within a matter of hours after the climactic events which mark the end of the narrative past." Although no evidence explicitly supports or controverts this claim, Marks joins Trachtenberg as one of the few to explore the problems of Huck's divergent roles. See "The Making of a Humorist: The Narrative Strategy of *Huckleberry Finn*," *Journal of Narrative Technique* 12 (Fall 1982):140. See also Trachtenberg, "The Form of Freedom," p. 966. John Seelye argues for a more damning but less problematic view than the one I develop, accusing the author Huck of withholding the novel's secrets and thereby becoming compelled despite himself to "live a lie." See "The Craft of Laughter: Abominable Showmanship and Huckleberry Finn," *Thalia* 4 (1981):19–25.

13 See *Adventures of Huckleberry Finn*, ed. Leo Marx (Indianapolis: Bobbs-Merrill, 1967), p. 174, fn. 1. For further discussion of this point, see Janet Holmgren McKay, *Narration and Discourse in American Realistic Fiction* (Philadelphia: University of Pennsylvania Press, 1982), pp. 145, 167.

14 Janet Holmgren McKay nicely observes Huck's play on such words as "deffersit," and his eye-dialect misspellings of "onkores" for "encores" and "diseased" for "deceased," but these reveal for her only Mark Twain's controlling influence, not Huck's authorial intrusions (p. 177). See also Carrington, *Dramatic Unity*, pp. 115–16.

15 Richard Bridgman has developed this point in *Colloquial Style*, pp. 87–92.

16 Joanna Wilks responds similarly to the news that her sister may have the "pluribus-unum mumps" – Huck's deception to keep the girls from the Duke and the King – with the ambiguous, " 'Shucks, and stay fooling around here when we could all be having good times in England whilst we was waiting to find out whether Mary Jane's got it or not?' "

17 Daniel Hoffman offers an argument directly counter to this in *Form and Fable in American Fiction* (New York: Oxford University Press, 1961), pp. 317–42.

18 For another assessment of Huck's "Providence" which assumes from this contradiction that Mark Twain "used" Huck, see J. R. Boggan, "That Slap, Huck, Did It Hurt?" *English Language Notes* 1 (March 1964):212–14.

19 In this same brief passage, Jim agrees to Tom's plan because he wants " 'no trouble in de house' " – a line that recalls Huck's earlier justification for putting up with the two confidence man: ". . . what you want, above all things, on a raft, is for everybody to be satisfied."

20 Although absent from the novel for thirty chapters, Tom is repeatedly invoked by Huck; see Chapters 8, 12, 28, 32, and 34. Louis D. Rubin, Jr., has similarly aligned Tom with Huck, though he finally does not see the two as similarly motivated. See Rubin, *Teller*, esp. pp. 77–8.

21 In a curious way, the issues at work in the story resonate through the novel – two accounts vying for authority. And notably, the assumption that the true mother speaks for the child by relinquishing her claim is never tested. This opens the possibility of a somewhat perverse alternative reading that is never excluded: At the last minute, the false testifier rather than the true mother recants, and thereby wins the child. Peter Seitz, in fact, has argued that "the harlot who prevailed in the case shrewdly took the measure of Solomon and decided that he was what would now be called a 'bleeding heart' – that is, a 'pushover' for a clever but insincere ploy. Her ploy was not as disinterested as Solomon assumed but rather was a deceptive stratagem to win the case." See "Strictly Arbitrary: What Do Arbitrators Do?" *American Scholar* 53 (Autumn 1984):514.

Reading *Huckleberry Finn:* The Rhetoric of Performed Ideology

STEVEN MAILLOUX

*A*DVENTURES *of Huckleberry Finn,* reviews of the novel, national party platforms, your morning newspaper, this essay — all these texts participate in the ongoing conversation of American culture. Kenneth Burke once described this conversation in the following way:

> Imagine that you enter a parlor. You come late. When you arrive, others have long preceded you, and they are engaged in a heated discussion, a discussion too heated for them to pause and tell you exactly what it is about. . . . You listen for a while, until you decide that you have caught the tenor of the argument; then you put in your oar. Someone answers; you answer him; another comes to your defense; another aligns himself against you, to either the embarrassment or gratification of your opponent, depending upon the quality of your ally's assistance. However, the discussion is interminable. The hour grows late, you must depart. And you do depart, with the discussion still vigorously in progress.[1]

This little fable depicts the cultural conversation as a series of rhetorical exchanges, with people constantly asserting, questioning, answering, defending, and sometimes changing their positions. It is an unending discussion, which begins before any individual participant joins in and continues long after he or she leaves the room. Burke's fable contains argumentative battles, rhetorical allies and enemies, and struggles for persuasive power. So that we don't take this *too* seriously, he also supplies a slightly Twainian twist in the ironic deflation of the verbal contests by placing them in a genteel parlor setting.

Burke's fable of rhetorical politics will prove useful for framing my analysis of *Huckleberry Finn.* In this essay I will examine the cultural conversation in and around Twain's novel, paying particular attention to the ideological rhetoric of the text and the way its arguments relate both to political quarrels of the 1880s and to academic discussions in the twentieth century. The first section locates *Huckleberry Finn* within the debates over racism after the end of Reconstruction, when the novel was first published; the second deals with the critical arguments of modern literary study when the novel was endlessly interpreted. Rhetoric – as persuasive argument and figurative language – will be the focus throughout.

We can think of *ideologies* as defining positions within the cultural conversation. Ideologies – like capitalism and socialism, abolition and white supremacy – are sets of ideas serving specific political interests in a particular historical context, and these ideas appear in the cultural conversation as strategic arguments and rhetorical figures. Literature's relation to all this is quite complex. A literary text can be a topic in the discussion, or it can be a participant who is motivated by and has effects on the conversation. As a participant, a literary text can take up the ideological rhetoric of its historical moment – the rhetoric of political speeches, newspaper editorials, book reviews, scholarly treatises, and so forth – and place it on a fictional stage. Readers thus become spectators at a rhetorical performance, and sometimes, as in *Huckleberry Finn*, they also become actors in the drama they are watching.[2]

We will see that the ideological drama of *Huckleberry Finn* relies for its success as much on the reader's participation as it does on Twain's script. The celebrated humor of the various narratives in the book – its histories, dreams, fictions, and elaborate lies – depends on the reader's perception of both the fictional speaker's purpose and the discrepancy between his tale and the "truth" as the reader understands it. Similarly, the humor and often the ideological point of the novel's many staged arguments – verbal disputes, Socratic dialogues, inner debates, and polemical monologues – rely upon the reader's ability to recognize patterns of false argumentation, especially by identifying the dubious authorities to which the arguments appeal: superstition, clichéd romanticism, institutionalized morality, and ultimately racist ideology. The irreverence of Twain's humor, for which he was often criticized, is only the most visible part of his more general attack on social authority, an attack that *Huckleberry Finn* carries out through a relentless questioning of *rhetorical* authorities that serve ideologically dubious ends. Again and again, the dramatized arguments make the reader laugh because the rhetorical authorities invoked appear as ridiculous confidence tricks that society plays on the individual.

The figure of the con man nicely overstates the nature of the rhetorical exchanges filling *Huckleberry Finn:* This kind of trickster is a self-interested rhetorician and a greedy manipulator. For a con to work, the mark must be convinced by the con man's visual and verbal rhetoric. Actual truth is irrelevant; what counts is successful persuasion about the truth. But the confidence man is not interested in simply performing tricks for the fun of it. He plays his game for a reason: He seeks to turn rhetorical exchanges into economic ones, to transform impassioned rhetoric into cold cash. The confidence man thus attempts not only to convince, to affect belief, but also to modify actions for his own benefit.[3] With this deceptive figure of the con man as our guide, we can turn to the staged arguments that the confidence trick exploits but does not exhaust. These arguments in the novel are ultimately part of a larger conversation taking place in America during the 1880s.

Ideological Rhetoric in 1885

I reckon I had better black my face, for in these Eastern States niggers are [judged] considerably better than white people.
  – S. L. Clemens to Jane Lampton Clemens, August 24, 1853

Report of the Debate had at Huckleberry Hollow, S.C., on the proposition to organize & institute The Society for the Propagation of Esthetic & Intellectual Culture. Let the dispute arise over the *name* – & break up in a row & bloodshed without getting further. Let it begin in a lofty & courtly parliamentary style of dignity, with some chief person . . . who simply wants "Religious" substituted for "Aesthetic," & supports his motion by a dignified but sophomoric speech. Two parties spring up – one for Religious, the other for Aesthetic – & as the debate gradually warms up, the drop into the most magnificent profanity & the most opulent & imaginative obscenity & finally have a fight.
  – Clemens, Notebook, July 18, 1879[4]

Huckleberry Finn appeared in February 1885 in the midst of a heated political quarrel over the absence of debate on the "race question." By the formal end of Reconstruction in 1877, a reunited nation had turned its rhetorical attention to matters other than those that had separated the states during the Civil War. This national change of subject included the North's relative silence on the race problem, which allowed the southern states to deal with the emancipated slaves on sectional rather than national terms and to roll back Reconstruction attempts to guarantee the blacks their political and civil rights. By 1885 the ideological rhetoric of white supremacy, uncontested by the North, dominated southern politics and eventually became institutionalized in state laws regulating relations between the white and black races.[5] Into this rhetorical context came the voice of George Washington Cable, popular southern author of *Old Creole Days* and *The Grandissimes*. From November 1884 to February 1885, Cable joined his friend Mark Twain on a widely publicized and highly successful reading tour through several northern and border states. In late December during the tour, *Century Magazine* published Cable's controversial attempt to reopen the debate on the race question. "The Freedman's Case in Equity" would have been controversial enough if its author had been a northerner, but as an essay written in the early 1880s by a citizen of Louisiana, its polemical argument was almost unthinkable.

Cable begins by claiming, "The greatest social problem before the American people today is, as it has been for a hundred years, the presence among us of the negro."[6] Yet, for all its importance, this problem is no longer discussed. There is an "absence of intellectual and moral debate" as the North, "weary of strife," has "thrown the whole matter over to the States of the South." Unfortunately, most southerners share an attitude that works, "to maintain a purely arbitrary superiority of all whites over all blacks." Cable goes on to analyze this ideology of white supremacy, which perpetuates the power of the ruling race by defining blacks as "an alien, menial, and dangerous class." This ideological definition of the ex-slave allows the southerner to justify his abridgement of the freedman's liberties. The result: a social system based on distinctions and separations that are "crude, invidious, humiliating, and tyrannous." Cable continues: "Nothing is easier to show than that these distinctions on the line of color are really made not from any necessity, but simply for their own sake – to preserve the old arbitrary supremacy of the master class over the menial."

This critique of southern ideology and social practice had an immediate effect. Deluged by letters attacking the essay, the *Century* editors invited a response from Henry W. Grady, editor of the Atlanta *Constitution*. Acknowledging that "the South has been silent" nationally on the "negro question," Grady proposed to break that silence and "speak the mind of the South."[7] He strongly rejects Cable's "suggestion of the social intermingling of the races." The hierarchy of white over black, which Cable found so invidious and arbitrary, Grady identifies as both healthy and natural. For Cable, the racial distinction is as unjust as it is unnecessary; but for Grady this same distinction is not only justified, it is the foundation of a stable society. He argues that the separation of the races is required by an "instinct that gathers each race about itself." But if there were no such racial instinct, he continues, it would have had to be invented. "Without it, there might be a breaking down of all lines of division and a thorough intermingling of whites and blacks." The racial separation must be preserved because its loss would lead to "the disorganization of society" and "an internecine war." Increasing the decibel level of his rhetoric, Grady embeds his racist ideology in argument and figure: "The whites, at any cost and at any hazard, would maintain the clear integrity and dominance of the Anglo-Saxon blood. . . . Even if the vigor and volume of the Anglo-Saxon blood would enable it to absorb the African current, and after many generations recover its own strength and purity, not all the powers of earth could control the unspeakable horrors that would wait upon the slow process of clarification." (As we will see, both the racist argument and its figuring as separated river currents appear in the rhetoric of *Huckleberry Finn*.) In calmer tones, Grady assesses the "separate" but "equal" accommodations for blacks throughout the South, and ends with a plea that the South be left alone to solve the race problem: "this implies the clear and unmistakable domination of the white race in the South. The assertion of that is simply the assertion of the right of character, intelligence, and property to rule. It is simply saying that the responsible and stead-fast element in the community shall control, rather than the irre-sponsible and migratory." These final sentences confirm Cable's assertion about the ideology of white supremacy: The racist in-terpretation of the freedman's nature requires that blacks remain "an alien, menial, and dangerous class" properly subjugated to perpetual white authority.

Into this highly charged and polarized argument came *Huckle-berry Finn,* and its relation to the renewed debate was more than topical. *Century Magazine* had published an extract in the same issue as "The Freedman's Case in Equity," and Twain regularly read to audiences from the novel during his tour with Cable. In-deed, the passages Twain chose to read were often those that most directly involved his humorous critique of white supremacist ide-ology, a critique carried out through Twain's rhetorical manipula-tion of his readers. To investigate the novel's rhetoric is to unfold its complicated nature as ideological performance. By staging rhe-torical exchanges – in the story and with his readers – Twain maneuvered his audience to cooperate with him in this perfor-mance. As we trace the progression of Twain's strategies, we will follow the reader through a series of reading events that encourage him or her to take a stance on the rhetorical authorities invoked and ultimately on a society's ideological politics.

The playful early episodes with Tom Sawyer's gang rehearse the reader for this critical role. In Chapter 2, as the gang debates its plan for "robbery and murder," Tom appeals to his authoritative knowledge of " 'pirate books and robber books.' " He convinces his followers that they must not only kill and steal but also "'ran-som'" their victims. When Tom admits that he doesn't know what ransoming means, a gang member objects, " 'But how can we do it if we don't know what it is?' " and Tom answers, " 'Why blame it all, we've *got* to do it. Don't I tell you it's in the books? Do you want to go to doing different from what's in the books, and get things all muddled up?' " The argument continues as Tom contrives a defi-nition of "ransom" – keeping hostages until they're dead – and then again invokes his authoritative reading of adventure books in response to the question, " 'Why can't a body take a club and ransom them as soon as they get here?' " In exasperation, Tom replies, " 'Because it ain't in the books so – that's why. . . . Don't you reckon that the people that made the books knows what's the correct thing to do?' " All this is innocent fun, imaginative play among boys, and it is amusing in its way. But the dialogue is more than just entertainment; it also serves as part of the reader's rhetorical training. For the humor to work, the reader must recognize not only the generic misreading of adventure stories as conduct books, but also the rhetorical appeal to a false authority followed blindly. Mastering this early and simpler lesson encourages the reader to question rhetorical authorities invoked later. These subsequent arguments involve more consequential misinterpretations, which the reader must call into question for the humor to be released and the ideological point made.

Next follows an argument in Chapter 3 that is actually an inner debate over the effectiveness of prayer. This debate within Huck begins: "I say to myself, if a body can get anything they pray for, why don't Deacon Winn get back the money he lost on pork? . . . No, says I to myself, there ain't nothing in it." Before the reader has a chance to agree or disagree, the widow corrects Huck's misreading of Christian doctrine: "I went and told the Widow Douglas about it, and she said the thing a body could get by praying for it was 'spiritual gifts.' " At most, Twain is satirizing selfish misinterpretations of Christian teaching here. No serious criticism of institutional religion seems intended. In fact, the Widow's explanation of these "spiritual gifts" gives a positive reading to at least one aspect of Christian ideology. Huck accepts the Widow's meaning of "prayer" but rejects its value: "she told me what she meant" by "spiritual gifts" – "I must help other people, and do everything I could for other people, and look out for them all the time, and never think about myself. . . . I went out in the woods and turned it over in my mind a long time, but I couldn't see no advantage about it – except for the other people – so at last I reckoned I wouldn't worry about it any more, but let it go." The irony, of course, is that what Huck here denies in words he later affirms in action. But at the moment, the reader is simply called on to laugh at Huck's misunderstandings and the boyish egoism of his arguments.

The innocent playfulness continues when Tom returns. He misreads *Don Quixote* and thereby convinces his gang that what they see is not what they'll get. Reading *Don Quixote* nonironically, he cites Part 1, Chapter 18, as proof that enemy magicians have turned "A-rabs" and elephants into a Sunday school class to frustrate Tom's gang.[8] His concluding insult for the unbeliever appeals to his own expertise and will be echoed later by Huck with more serious ideological implications. As Huck continues to challenge his claims, Tom says, " 'Shucks, it ain't no use to talk to you, Huck Finn. You don't seem to know anything, somehow – perfect saphead.' " Here, as later, the reader recognizes that the insult comically boomerangs; it is not Huck but Tom who is misguided.

Later, argumentative appeals to superstition work in similar ways. The reader is cast in the role of the critical listener, participating in the fun by recognizing the questionable authority of the interpretations invoked. But up to this point, little political weight has been attached to any of these rhetorical performances. The satire remains directed at the misreaders more than at the ideas misread. Still unexamined is the power of ideologies to misinterpret in a rhetorically self-interested way.

This situation now changes abruptly. Without skipping a comedic beat, Twain slides his readers comfortably into the role of ideological critics, the role they will play for the rest of the novel. In Chapter 6, after the law prevents him from getting hold of his son's money, Pap Finn launches into a wild monologue violently attacking the " 'govment' " where a " 'man can't get his rights.' " Pap's speech shifts into a racist diatribe when he bitterly complains about news that a visiting " 'free nigger' " from Ohio could actually " '*vote*, when he was at home. Well, that let me out. Thinks I, what is the country a-coming to? It was 'lection day, and I was just about to go and vote, myself, if I warn't too drunk to get there; but when they told me there was a State in this country where they'd let that nigger vote, I drawed out. I says I'll never vote agin.' " The satire of the poor white approaches silly burlesque but pulls back in time to allow the righteous indignation of the speech to serve as the reader's first extended introduction to the ideology of white supremacy in *Huckleberry Finn*. The entertaining monologue requires little rhetorical work from the reader. The racism remains on the surface of the discourse, and the striking contrast between the speaker's ethos and his well-educated black target — " 'a p'fessor in a college' " — makes the ideological point, one that prepares the way for the more interesting rhetorical performances to follow.

The rhetoric of the arguments staged later asks readers to perform increasingly more challenging tasks: They must not merely witness but contribute to a debate or judge its winner. In Chapter 14, for example, Huck and Jim argue over interpreting the biblical account of Solomon. The debate begins when Jim questions whether anyone with a million wives could possibly be wise. Huck appeals to the authority of Widow Douglas and the traditional interpretation in claiming that Solomon was indeed the wisest of men. Jim contradicts Huck, citing the story " "bout dat chile dat he 'uz gwyne to chop in two.' " Comparing half a child to half of a dollar bill, Jim asks, " 'what use is a half a chile?' " and argues that the story doesn't show how wise Solomon was but, rather, demonstrates his *lack* of wisdom. Huck doesn't explicitly provide an alternative reading for the story; he simply rejects Jim's: " 'But hang it, Jim, you've clean missed the point — blame it, you've missed it a thousand mile.' " Jim counters by elaborating his reading a bit more: " 'Doan' talk to *me* 'bout yo' pints. I reck'n I knows sense when I sees it; en dey ain't no sense in sich doin's as dat. . . . [D]e man dat think he kin settle a 'spute 'bout a whole chile wid a half a chile doan' know enough to come in out'n de rain.' " Again, Huck does not respond by presenting a counterreading; he simply reiterates his objection to Jim's interpretation: " 'But I tell you you don't get the point.' "

But what *is* the point of the biblical story? Readers must supply it themselves: The incident is part of a narrative that tries to demonstrate Solomon's great wisdom. Jim doesn't miss the rhetorical point of the story; he is arguing that the story fails to make the point. As readers supply the traditional reading, they participate in the debate's staging, and this participation is the basis of its humor for them. But the dramatized argument is funny not because it displays Jim's ignorance but because of the discrepancy between the authoritative interpretation and Jim's surprising rereading. Indeed, Jim shows himself to be quite adept at interpretive rhetoric when, after first brushing aside the hermeneutic concept of " 'the point' " of a story, he coopts the concept and argues that " 'de *real*

pint is down furder – it's down deeper.' " This deeper point is that
Solomon has so many children he doesn't care about any individual one. " 'A chile er two, mo' er less, warn't no consekens to
Sollermun.' " This rhetorical move – going beyond your adver-
sary's superficial interpretation – neatly returns the conversation
to its beginning, the topic of Solomon's many wives.

Twain again displays Jim's rhetorical skill in the argument that
immediately follows. In this performance, the reader participates
by deciding who wins the debate. Jim questions the obvious state-
ment that it makes sense for a Frenchman to speak French, and
Huck responds by initiating his own version of a Socratic dialogue:

> "Looky here, Jim, does a cat talk like we do?"
> "No, a cat don't."
> "Well, does a cow?"
> "No, a cow don't, nuther."
> "Does a cat talk like a cow, or a cow talk like a cat?"
> "No, dey don't."
> "It's natural and right for 'em to talk different from each other,
> ain't it?"
> " 'Course."
> "And ain't it natural and right for a cat and a cow to talk different
> from *us?*"
> "Why, mos' sholy it is."
> "Well, then, why ain't it natural and right for a *Frenchman* to talk
> different from us? – you answer me that."

Instead of answering with the generally accepted fact, the logical
conclusion to which Jim and the reader have been led by Huck's
argument, Jim retaliates with his own Socratic dialogue modeled
after Huck's:

> "Is a cat a man, Huck?"
> "No."
> "Well, den, dey ain't no sense in a cat talkin' like a man. Is a cow
> a man? – er is a cow a cat?"
> "No, she ain't either of them."
> "Well, den, she ain't got no business to talk like either one er the
> yuther of 'em. Is a Frenchman a man?"
> "Yes."
> "*Well*, den! Dad blame it, why doan' he *talk* like a man? – you
> answer me *dat!*"

Who wins the debate? Jim has skillfully replicated the pattern of Huck's argument, and by burying a false premise – "All men should speak English" – he beats Huck at his own game. At first, the rhetorical exchange appears to emphasize Jim's ignorance, but by the time readers get to the end, they realize that the staged argument demonstrates Jim's rhetorical ingenuity. Twain emphasizes the ideological irony of this performance when he has Huck conclude the exchange: "I see it warn't no use wasting words – you can't learn a nigger to argue. So I quit." Of course, readers reject the racist slur as a rationalization. They know Huck gives up because he has lost the argument: It is precisely because Jim *has* learned to argue by imitating Huck that he reduces his teacher to silence. Far from demonstrating Jim's inferior knowledge, the debate dramatizes his argumentative superiority, and in doing so makes a serious ideological point through a rhetoric of humor.

These rhetorical performances, then, function simultaneously as amusing entertainments *and* as ideological critiques of white supremacy. Early readers of *Huckleberry Finn*, we know, appreciated the special humor of these dialogues. Twain included "King Sollermun" and "How come a Frenchman doan' talk like a man?" in his 1884–5 reading tour. A warning from Cable had emphasized their direct relevance to the race problem. Asked for suggestions about which passages to include in their program, Cable replied that "King Sollermun" was "enough by itself to immortalize its author," but he raised a question about one of the program titles, "Can't learn a nigger to argue." He cautioned, "In the text, whether on the printed page or in the reader's utterances the phrase is absolutely without a hint of grossness; but alone on a published programme, it invites discreditable conjectures of what the context may be."[9] Twain apparently agreed with Cable because he accepted his partner's new title, "How come a Frenchman doan' talk like a man?" Afterward, during the last few weeks of the tour, the "Twins of Genius" could not help remaining sensitive to the race issue when the *Century* published "The Freedman's Case in Equity."

On stage and in print, Jim's two rhetorical performances were potentially just as subversive of racist ideology as Cable's less humorous and more explicit attack. But their impact is perhaps best seen by contrasting the two dialogues with similar rhetorical performances that have an opposite ideological effect. In October 1869 Clemens's *Buffalo Express* published an item that quotes a "darkey's account of a sermon": "Well, sahs, de sermon was upon de miricles of de loaves and fishes. De ministers said how de 7000 loaves and de 5000 fishes divided between de twelve apostles; and de miricle was, dat they didn't bust!"[10] The ignorance revealed in the black's misreading is the only source of humor in the sketch. By contrast, Jim's rereading of the King Solomon episode illustrates his ingenuity and skill in interpretive argument. The result is that a reader's racist ideology is, in the former case, reinforced but, in the latter, contradicted.

In November 1869 the *Buffalo Express* published another dialogue between black characters:

> "I say, Baz, where do dat comet rise?"
> "It rises in the forty-six meridian ob de frigid zodiac, as laid down in the comic almanac."
> "Well, where does it set, Baz?"
> "Set! you black fool! It don't set nowhere. When it gets tired of shining it goes into its hole."[11]

Again, the dialogue appeals to racist stereotypes. As Arthur G. Pettit has argued, these early sketches depend on readers enjoying the "ignorance, superstition, simplicity, gullibility" of the black characters for "what little 'humor' distinguishes them."[12] The contrast to Jim's rhetorical victory in *Huckleberry Finn* is striking. While the ideological presence of white racism permeates both early and later rhetorical performances and is in both a necessary ingredient of the humor, in the latter case racist ideology is turned inside out.

In the inner debates staged at the ideological center of *Huckleberry Finn*, Twain again asks the reader to judge the rhetorical authority and help make the ideological point. Huck's first internal argument in Chapter 16 sets the stage for later ones. The two disputants are his socialized conscience and his private feelings, primarily his sense of loyalty. Throughout the novel's critical history, this inner conflict has usually been conceived as a struggle between a racist ideology imposed from without and Huck's natural goodness within.[13] Viewed rhetorically, the first round of the debate is won by Huck's conscience when it breaks down every one of his justifications for helping Jim escape: "I tried to make out to myself that *I* warn't to blame, because *I* didn't run Jim off from his rightful owner; but it warn't no use, conscience up and says, every time, 'But you knowed he was running from his freedom, and you could a paddled ashore and told somebody.' " Finally, Huck gives up and says to his conscience, "Let up on me – it ain't too late, yet – I'll paddle ashore at the first light, and tell." And so he tries but discovers he "warn't man enough – hadn't the spunk of a rabbit." Huck can't condone his act of protecting Jim. He must interpret it as weakness because his conscience has initially won the inner debate by appealing to the authority of racist ideology, an ideology so deeply internalized that Huck accuses himself of being a potential accessory to a strange kind of kidnapping: "Here was this nigger which I had as good as helped to run away, coming right out flat-footed and saying he would steal his [enslaved] children – children that belonged to a man I didn't even know; a man that hadn't ever done me no harm." Convinced of his wickedness by a persuasive conscience, Huck can't help condemning himself. But as in the other staged debates, the reader recognizes the false nature of the winning argument – its appeal to false authority – and once again supplies the ideological point and the basis for the episode's ironic humor.

The rhetorical follow-up to Huck's "failure" is one of many instances when Huck takes on the role of confidence man. Playing this role again and again, Huck repeatedly figures the nature of the rhetorical exchanges throughout the novel. In this particular case, he protects Jim by persuading the slave hunters to believe a fiction that they themselves supply. From Huck's deliberately hesitant answer to their questions, the slave hunters infer that Huck's "father" is much sicker than he's letting on: " 'Your pap's got the small-pox,' " they cry backing away from the raft, " 'and you know it precious well.' " In an ironic inversion of the reader's past performances, the hunters think they supply the truth that corrects Huck's lie when actually they supply the lie that covers the truth Huck wants to hide. Huck orchestrates the scene perfectly. Not only is the main purpose of the con achieved – Jim is protected –

but, as in many other cases, the rhetorical exchange becomes an economic exchange as well: To assuage their guilt for abandoning the boy, the hunters leave him two twenty-dollar gold pieces. Thus enriched, Huck soon returns to the debate between his public conscience and his private benevolence.

But this traditional characterization of the internal argument oversimplifies the rhetorical situation. Viewing Huck's conflict as a debate between racist ideology and Huck's natural goodness may be a useful way to get at the ideological point of his inner struggle, but it is not very helpful in capturing the rhetorical dynamics of the internal dialogue. Indeed, the critical history's habitual way of characterizing the debate is misleading because it identifies both rhetorical stands as primarily *ethical* positions, and this is simply not the case.[14] Only Huck's public conscience cites reasons based on the ethical opposition between good and bad. In contrast, Huck's natural "goodness" bases its argument on pragmatic considerations about feeling happy and about actions being troublesome, considerations that tend to break down simple distinctions between good and evil. Incapable of turning Jim in, Huck describes himself as "feeling bad and low, because I knowed very well I had done wrong. . . . Then I thought a minute, and says to myself, hold on, – s'pose you'd a done right and give Jim up; would you felt better than what you do now? No, says I, I'd feel bad – I'd feel just the same way I do now. Well, then, says I, what's the use you learning to do right, when it's troublesome to do right and ain't no trouble to do wrong, and the wages is just the same? I was stuck. I couldn't answer that. So I reckoned I wouldn't bother no more about it, but after this always do whichever come handiest at the time."

Huck's personal pragmatism reduces his public conscience to silence, and the rhetorical triumph is reversed. But this has been a debate not between ideologies – racism and, say abolition – but between public morality and private feeling. Any ideological coloring has been supplied by the reader, who – as the critical history demonstrates – judges Huck's conscience as racist and his feelings as nonracist and therein naturally "good." Out of this reader-produced distinction emerges the debate's more complex ironies. For Huck's natural "goodness" wins the supposedly ethical debate with an amoral argument, one that silences his public conscience but ignores its appeal to racist ideology. Not only must readers supply the relevant ideological critique, not only must they reject the continued appeal to false authority, they must also recognize that "goodness" triumphs by arguing for amorality! This humorous rhetoric works because the reader has become as active in the ideological performance as are Huck's conscience and feelings.

The climactic argument in Chapter 31 simply restages these earlier inner debates in less complicated and more powerful form. But before readers arrive at this rhetorical climax, they must make their way through a different set of ideological issues. The focus shifts from race to class, from a critique of white supremacy to an ideological performance of Twain's bourgeois liberalism, with its simultaneous attack on aristocratic privilege and mob rule. As Louis J. Budd points out, this ideological position can be characterized as Manchester liberalism, which rejected authoritarianism and protected the rights of the people. But "the people" were defined as the propertied middle class, and this liberal ideology was no less suspicious of the unwashed masses than of the gentry elite.[15] Thus, after the dramatized debates that rhetorically critique racism, Chapters 17 through 30 enlarge the ideological stage to enact a liberal attack on aristocracy – southern, British, and French – and on the commoner – primarily poor whites. Certainly the middle class does not escape censure here, but its shortcomings appear minor by comparison.

In these chapters, the figure of the confidence man returns with renewed rhetorical vigor as the fake king and fake duke work their persuasive magic in con after con. By playing up the "tears and flapdoodle" of the con man's speeches at the camp meeting and the Wilks funeral, Twain forces the reader to see the extreme gullibility of the citizens as they are parted from their money.[16] But if the middle class is satirized for its sentimentality and credulity, the author saves his more serious condemnation for the violence of the southern gentry and poor whites. This is not surprising. Nineteenth-century liberalism placed ultimate value on individual rights, and thus feuds and lynchings were ideological anathemas in their violent denial of the right to life. Twain himself might have said: "A fly bothers me, I kill it; you kill what bothers you. If I had not killed the fly, it would have been *out of pure liberalism:* I am liberal in order not to be a killer."[17] Again, *Huckleberry Finn* rhetorically enacts and leads its readers to enact its ideological critique. Two examples will suffice to show the connection Twain makes between class violence and persuasive power.

In Chapter 18, Huck describes the feud between the Grangerfords and Shepherdsons, two "clan[s] of aristocracy" that were "high-toned, and well-born, and rich and grand." Explaining the feud to Huck, Buck Grangerford appeals to tradition in justifying the constant killing. He defines a "feud" with a narrative: "'A man has a quarrel with another man, and kills him; then that other man's brother kills *him;* then the other brothers, on both sides, goes for one another; then the *cousins* chip in – and by-and-by everybody's killed off, and there ain't no more feud. But it's kind of slow, and takes a long time.'" But when Huck asks about the feud's origin, he finds that no one knows "now what the row was about in the first place." Buck sees no problem with his appeal to this dubious rhetorical authority – a tradition of self-perpetuating murder originating in an unknown argument. Buck sees no problem, but of course the reader does.

But should the reader also notice that the feud is simply the original lost argument dramatized in physical violence? Certainly a later rhetorical performance shows another close relation between verbal and brute force. In Chapter 22, Sherburn's speech to the lynch mob shifts the critique from gentry to poor whites but stays focused on violence. Sherburn notes how easy it is for a crowd to transform itself into a lynch party. All that's needed is a leader's persuasion and a mob's cowardice. "'The average man don't like trouble and danger. *You* don't like trouble and danger. But if only *half* a man – like Buck Harkness, there – shouts "Lynch him, lynch him!" you're afraid to back down – afraid you'll be found out to be what you are – *cowards.*'" But if the rhetorical point here is that effective rhetoric can lead to violence, it is also the case that Sherburn's speech itself prevents violence from taking place, at least temporarily. Besides criticizing mob rule, then, this speech displays the power of rhetoric, whether for good or ill, whether for deflecting or inciting violence.

Twain had introduced his liberal critique of poor whites much earlier in presenting Pap's racist speech (Chap. 6). The difference between the earlier and later rhetorical performances is that Pap's diatribe illustrates only the inversion of white supremacist ideology. His speech humorously (if too obviously) demonstrates that the black professor is more qualified to vote than the white drunkard. But in the later lynch mob sequence, the implied violence of Pap's words becomes the issue, and the scene dramatizes not the undesirability of universal suffrage but the actual dangers of mob rule and the power of rhetoric to manipulate the masses.

Although the performance of bourgeois liberalism dominates the rhetorical stage in these middle chapters, the critique of white racism does not simply wait in the wings. It reappears, for example, in Chapter 26 when Huck tries to convince Mary Jane Wilks that British servants are worse off than American slaves. But the novel's ideological climax takes place in the famous inner debate of Chapter 31, where Huck wrestles with the question of whether to rescue Jim. The argument is simple in its rhetorical lines: on one side, Huck's socially imposed conscience; on the other, his feelings of affection for and loyalty to Jim. At first, his conscience appeals not only to racist ideology but also to that ideology's use of Christianity in support of slavery. Huck has no defense. Believing that "people that acts as I'd been acting about that nigger goes to everlasting fire," Huck decides to write Jim's owner that her runaway slave can be found imprisoned at the Phelps' farm. "Washed clean of sin for the first time . . . ever," he contemplates how close he had "come to being lost and going to hell." Then, with his conscience's guard down, Huck's feelings make their persuasive counterattack. Thinking over his trip down the river with Jim, Huck finds that he "couldn't seem to strike no places to harden me against him, but only the other kind." Despite himself, Huck begins piling up Jim's many acts of friendship as good reasons for changing his mind. He looks at the letter to Jim's owner, studies a minute, then says, "All right, then, I'll *go* to hell," and tears up the paper.

In the text, Huck's feelings triumph over his conscience; friendship wins out over racism. Only in the reader's mind is the victor Huck's "natural goodness." It is also important to recognize that the rhetorical victory does not change Huck's ideological beliefs in the slightest, only his actions. As many critics have observed, Huck's continued acceptance of racist ideology guarantees that he will misread his decision as "wicked." It is the reader who applies the moral label of "good" to the outcome of the inner debate. Huck's appeal to the false authority of racist ideology once again ironically enacts a critique that the reader helps perform.

Difference is the essence of debate, and so it is no accident that the debates staged throughout *Huckleberry Finn* are almost always arguments over *differences:* differences between fact and fiction, good and bad, wise men and fools, Americans and Frenchmen, servants and slaves. In one episode, raftsmen get "to talking about differences betwixt hogs, and their different kind of habits; and next about women and their different ways . . . and next about differences betwixt clear-water rivers and muddy-water ones." This last topic becomes a discussion of the specific differences between the Mississippi and Ohio rivers. One man claims that "the muddy Mississippi water was wholesomer to drink than the clear water of the Ohio." The group agrees and then talks "about how Ohio water didn't like to mix with Mississippi water" (Chap. 16). Of the many differences discussed in *Huckleberry Finn*, this last comes closest to figuring the novel's central concern, the ideologically produced differences between the races, and it recalls the river metaphor used by Grady in his racist response to Cable's *Century* essay.

Throughout *Huckleberry Finn*, dramatized arguments again and again break down all these differences or overturn their hierarchies. Wise men become fools, Frenchmen should talk like Americans, what is socially approved is morally reprehensible, the inferior slave is superior to his master. Although whites don't want to "mix" with blacks, at least one black man proves "wholesomer" than most whites. This turn exposes the black–white difference as an ideological imposition that in the progress of the narrative is slowly but surely undone. In the end, Huck discovers that Jim is actually "white inside." Although this is another of those sincere compliments that presupposes racism, it also works on the level of ideological figure to dismantle the opposition upon which that racism is based: Black and white become morally indistinguishable.[18]

Interpretive Rhetoric in 1985

> Men think they think upon great political questions, and they do; but they think with their party, not independently; they read its literature, but not that of the other side. . . . They swarm with their party, they feel with their party, they are happy in their party's approval.
> — Mark Twain, "Corn-Pone Opinions" (1901)
>
> America in 1985 (Negro supremacy — the whites under foot)
> — Clemens, Notebook, January 23, 1885[19]

Our reading of *Huckleberry Finn* has stopped short of the concluding "Evasion" episode, where Huck and Tom attempt to free Jim. Twain wrote this complicated scene to burlesque romantic adventure stories, stories that Tom invokes to authorize his convoluted rescue plans. But many readers have been decidedly unimpressed by the episode, complaining that it is too long and inappropriate, a disappointing ending to Twain's masterpiece. How can my rhetorical interpretation address this, the primary critical problem in readings of *Huckleberry Finn?* The question suggests two others: How did the interpretive problem develop as such? And what effect does that development have on any attempt at a solution? These questions will take us into the critical history in which Twain's life and novel have been publicly debated. Here we move from *Huckleberry Finn* as participant in the cultural conversation to the novel as topic within it, from the text talking to its being talked about.

To understand *Huckleberry Finn's* critical history, we must modify the fable discussed in my introduction. In Burke's parlor of cultural debate, the disputants participate in a heated discussion, "too heated for them to pause and tell [the latecomer] exactly what it is about."[20] In fact, the interpretive latecomers to *Huckleberry Finn* criticism find many disputants who will stop and give them the conversational lowdown, supplying ample if not disinterested information about the state of the discussion. Indeed, in a sense, a text's critical history is constantly writing (and rewriting) itself in public because of certain institutional practices within literary studies: the introductory summaries of past criticism in interpretive articles, bibliographic essays periodically surveying the state of scholarship, book reviews placing a book's argument in the context of ongoing critical debate, and collections of reprinted commentaries introduced by retellings of a text's critical history. Out of such institutional discourses emerge interpretive problems – often identified as such – that later critical rhetoric needs to address in order to stay relevant and persuasive. These publicized problems become part of the latecomer's crash course on the Twainian conversation, and soon he or she is able to dip in an argumentative oar and join the problem-solving debates.

In the 1980s this crash course emphasizes two episodes in the critical history: an initial debate over the author's life and a later argument over the form and value of his most important novel. Actually, these two episodes of the Twainian conversation are closely related, the historical problem of Twain's "wound" becoming the formalist problem of *Huckleberry Finn's* ending. In *The Ordeal of Mark Twain* (1920), Van Wyck Brooks introduces the first major problem for Twain scholarship by arguing that a commercial and genteel America had prevented Samuel Clemens from being the great writer he could have been.[21] Rather than criticize his society in a significant way, Twain succumbed to its crass materialism and stifling morality by becoming a mere humorist.

Applying his thesis to *Huckleberry Finn,* Brooks discovers the literary repetition of Twain's personal struggle. In Twain's inner life, the conventional citizen battled the rebelling writer; social conformity suppressed artistic individualism. In his novel, this battle becomes Huck's psychological struggle, "one between conscience and the law, on one side, and sympathy on the other." Brooks argues that "in the famous episode of Nigger Jim, 'sympathy,' the cause of individual freedom, wins." But if the conclict in *Huckleberry Finn* is simply the conflict in Mark Twain, the resolutions turn out to be quite different. Twain solves the conflict "successfully, he fulfills his desire, in the book, as an author can. In actual life he did not solve it at all; he surrendered."[22] And this surrender, Brooks claims, took the form of becoming a humorist. For Twain, humor was his compromise with social convention, a compromise forced on him by his need to conform, a compromise that suppressed his artistic spirit. He could have been a committed critic of his society. Instead, he becomes its clown.

The impassioned debate Brooks initiated continued for years. When at midcentury Lionel Trilling and T. S. Eliot commented on the ending of *Huckleberry Finn*, the problematic relation between humor and ideological seriousness remained. But in their analyses, the problem is translated from a biographical debate about Twain's life to a formalist quarrel over a text's unity.[23] The old question "Was humor Twain's escape from seriously criticizing his times?" is replaced by another: "Is the story of Jim's escape a farcical betrayal of *Huckleberry Finn's* earlier ideological critique?" As a historicist conversation surrounding Twain's work became a formalist discussion, the critical history often recorded this transformation. In 1962, for example, Lewis Leary concluded his introduction to *A Casebook on Mark Twain's Wound* with the observation that many critics "have turned to what seems today the legitimate province of literary criticism – concern with what a man wrote rather than why he wrote it."[24]

Thus did Trilling's and Eliot's formalist defense of *Huckleberry Finn's* conclusion begin shifting the set of problems addressed in Twain's critical history. But for any change of subject to occur, the conversational participants must recognize the shift and act accordingly. For a new debate to start, sides must be chosen in the argument and the topic must become generally accepted by those concerned. Leo Marx soon took this first step in his incisive "Mr. Eliot, Mr. Trilling, and *Huckleberry Finn*," where he attacked the claims made for the novel's formal unity.[25]

Marx argues that "to bring *Huckleberry Finn* to a satisfactory close, Clemens had to do more than find a neat device for ending a story. His problem, though it may never have occurred to him, was to invent an action capable of placing in focus the meaning of the journey down the Mississippi." And the meaning of the journey, according to Marx, is the "quest for freedom." Huck's "unpremeditated identification with Jim's flight from slavery is an unforgettable moment in American experience, and it may be said at once that any culmination of the journey which detracts from the urgency and dignity with which it begins will necessarily be unsatisfactory." Marx goes on to explain why the burlesque ending is indeed "unsatisfactory" in the extreme. Among other objections, he argues that "the slapstick tone jars with the underlying seriousness of the voyage"; that Huck unaccountably regresses into "Tom's helpless accomplice, submissive and gullible"; and that Jim undergoes a similar transformation into a "flat stereotype: the submissive stage–Negro." Worst of all, the ending diminishes Huck's heroic victory over the socially imposed morality justifying slavery.

With Marx's essay taking this first step, all that remained for the dispute over the ending to become a problem for the critical history was its incorporation into the discipline's later discourse on *Huckleberry Finn*. This was quickly accomplished by the long string of articles that took up the argument and by the many collections of reprinted essays that included the interpretations of Trilling, Eliot, and Marx. Future arguments did not remain exclusively within the bounds of formalism, but the formalist concentration on the text in and of itself continues to focus debate to the present day.

This, then, is the rhetorical context as *Huckleberry Finn* passes its centenary. My own ideological interpretation finds the critical history posing the problem of the ending and simultaneously laying out the possible solutions. Either the "evasion" episode contradicts what has gone before in the novel or it somehow fits in with it. If the former, it is an artistic failure; if the latter, it's really not a problem at all. One sure way for a new interpretation to join the debate is to choose a side. But a more effective critical strategy would be to show how the traditional solutions to the problem are not – as the critical history would have it – mutually exclusive. This strategy gives us the final step in my rhetorical interpretation: The "evasion" sequence *is* a problem, but it *does* fit in with the rest of the novel. Indeed, in order for the concluding chapters to work, readers must experience the episode as a problem while reading so that they can once again participate in the ideological performance.

Past interpretations repeatedly testify to this disconcerting experience as they record the many questions critics have posed about the ending: Is the characterization of Huck and Jim consistent with that in the river episodes? Does the farcical escape betray the earlier social criticism? Does the outlandish humor undermine the previous ideological seriousness? These and other questions particularize the problem in the reading experience as it is stated and restated in past criticism. What we have done here is to make the critical debate itself signify by presenting its questions as evidence of how troublesome readers have found reading the "Evasion" episode. From this perspective, the critical solutions to the problem, the specific positions taken in the debates, are less important than the fact that a problem was experienced in the first place.[26]

In my interpretation, the final clash between entertaining humor and ideological seriousness remains, with all its problematic obtrusiveness. But now the two attitudes are no longer simply positions argued for in the critical history; they are concerns developed in the reader's experience of the conclusion. Futhermore, if previously the text enacted its ideological critique *through* the humor, now it does so *despite* the farce. That is, in the novel's earlier staged arguments, the reader released the humor by identifying the grounds upon which the rhetorical performances were based. But at the end, readers must separate the comedy from the ideological point they have mastered. Either during or after reading the farce, they must realize that something is wrong, that there *is* a problem with the ending, one that the text will not help solve. But the text has created the problem insofar as readers have been persuaded to take the earlier humorous critiques of racism seriously. As a result, readers must decide whether the ending shows Twain's ideological retreat or his political realism, whether it contradicts his earlier attack on racism or deliberately represents the impossibility of the ex-slave's freedom. In a sense, it simply does not matter whether the interpretive and evaluative problem is resolved in Twain's favor or not. The fact that the problem appears at all testifies that the novel works, not as a formal unity but as a rhetorical performance in which the reader must participate in order to read at all.

In 1869 Clemens's *Buffalo Express* published a sketch, "A Rural Lesson in Rhetoric," in which a character advises a temperance lecturer to adapt his words to the understanding of his audience. The speaker is grateful for this, "the best lesson in rhetoric" he "ever received."[27] In *Huckleberry Finn* the author shapes not only individual words but whole speeches and dialogues to the abilities of his readers. For he depends throughout on his audience's help in establishing his novel's engaging humor and its ideological impact. But besides shaping his discourse, Twain rhetorically shapes his readers as well. I am not claiming, however, that the reader radically changes in the course of reading *Huckleberry Finn*. Rather, in depending on the reader's ability to critique false authority, Twain accomplishes a "training of the reader to see with his own eyes."[28] This training involves readers in becoming more rhetorically aware of the ideological issues they help raise throughout the novel. The very reason there is a problem with the ending is due to this training and to the reader's early encounters with the novel's ideological rhetoric, which then directs attention to the concluding interpretive problem. It is this effective rhetorical power, both humorous and serious, that makes *Huckleberry Finn* not only a successful novel but also an important voice in the unending conversation of American culture.

NOTES

1 Kenneth Burke, *The Philosophy of Literary Form* (Baton Rouge: Louisiana State University Press, 1941), pp. 110–11. I am indebted to the excellent discussion of Burke's fable in Frank Lentricchia, *Criticism and Social Change* (Chicago: University of Chicago Press, 1983), pp. 160–2.

2 For other analyses of *Huckleberry Finn* in terms of "performances," see James M. Cox, *Mark Twain: The Fate of Humor* (Princeton, N.J.: Princeton University Press, 1966), pp. 136–51, and the more extended use of the dramaturgical metaphor in George C. Carrington, Jr., *The Dramatic Unity of Huckleberry Finn* (Columbus: Ohio State University Press, 1976). For a discussion of Twain's audience, especially in relation to the subscription trade through which *Huckleberry Finn* was published, see Hamlin Hill, "Mark Twain: Audience and Artistry," *American Quarterly* 15 (Spring 1963):25–40. Also see Eileen Nixon Meredith, "Mark Twain and the Audience: A Rhetorical Study" (Ph.D. diss., Duke University, 1976).

3 For analyses of the confidence man in Twain's fiction generally, see Susan Kuhlmann, *Knave, Fool, and Genius: The Confidence Man as He*

Appears in Nineteenth-Century Fiction (Chapel Hill: University of North Carolina Press, 1973); Warwick Wadlington, *The Confidence Game in American Literature* (Princeton, N.J.: Princeton University Press, 1975); and Gary Lindberg, *The Confidence Man in American Literature* (New York: Oxford University Press, 1982).

4 Letter File, Mark Twain Papers, Bancroft Library, University of California, Berkeley, quoted in Arthur G. Pettit, *Mark Twain & the South* (Lexington: University Press of Kentucky, 1974), p. 23; *Mark Twain's Notebooks and Journals*, vol. 2, ed. Frederick Anderson, Lin Salamo, and Bernard L. Stein (Berkeley: University of California Press, 1975), pp. 332–33.

5 For a detailed examination of white supremacist ideology in southern arguments over politics, education, and labor during and after Reconstruction, see Claude H. Nolen, *The Negro's Image in the South: The Anatomy of White Supremacy* (Lexington: University of Kentucky Press, 1967). Of course, southern rhetoric had no monopoly on racist ideology; for an overview of northern racism, see Forrest G. Wood, *Black Scare: The Racist Response to Emancipation and Reconstruction* (Berkeley: University of California Press, 1970), pp. 1–16.

6 All quotations in this paragraph are taken from George W. Cable, "The Freedman's Case in Equity," *Century Magazine* 29 (January 1885):409–18.

7 All quotations in this paragraph (except the last) are taken from Henry W. Grady, "In Plain Black and White: A Reply to Mr. Cable," *Century Magazine* 29 (April 1885):909–17.

8 Olin H. Moore, "Mark Twain and Don Quixote," *PMLA* 37 (June 1922):337–8.

9 Cable to Clemens, October 25, 1884, reprinted in Guy A Cardwell, *Twins of Genius* (East Lansing: Michigan State College Press, 1953), pp. 104–5.

10 *Buffalo Express*, October 4, 1869, p. 2.

11 *Buffalo Express*, November 8, 1869, p. 2 (paragraphing modified).

12 Arthur G. Pettit, "Mark Twain and the Negro, 1867–69," *Journal of Negro History* 56 (April 1971):95.

13 Twain encourages this reading in an 1895 notebook entry, in which he refers to *Huckleberry Finn* as a book "where a sound heart & a deformed conscience come into collision & conscience suffers defeat" (Mark Twain Papers, Notebook 35, typescript p. 35).

14 The most interesting ethical restaging of the debate is Walter Blair's in *Mark Twain & Huckleberry Finn* (Berkeley: University of California Press, 1960), pp. 135–44, where he explains how Twain is carrying

on an argument with W. E. H. Lecky's *History of European Morals from Augustus to Charlemagne* (1869).

15 See Louis J. Budd, *Mark Twain: Social Philosopher* (Bloomington: Indiana University Press, 1962), esp. pp. 60, 68, 105. Budd's description of Twain's ideological commitments is much more convincing than the radical "left perspective" attributed to Twain by Michael Egan in *Mark Twain's Huckleberry Finn: Race, Class, and Society* (London: Sussex University Press, 1977), p. 66. Cf. Philip Foner, *Mark Twain: Social Critic* (New York: International Publishers, 1958).

16 Revisions in the extant manuscript indicate that Twain worked to increase the satire on the townspeople's weakness before the con man's rhetoric. As Walter Blair puts it, "By constantly making the king's language more vulgar and slangy, Mark makes the cheat's pretense more transparent, his victim's gullibility more stupid" (*Mark Twain and Huckleberry Finn*, p. 352). For the relevant revisions, see *Adventures of Huckleberry Finn (Tom Sawyer's Comrade) by Mark Twain: A Facsimile of the Manuscript*, vol. 1 (Detroit: Gale, 1983), pp. 149–50 (pp. 241–2 in the manuscript pagination).

17 Roland Barthes, *Roland Barthes*, trans. Richard Howard (New York: Hill and Wang, 1977), p. 117.

18 But while racial oppositions tend ideologically to collapse in *Huckleberry Finn*, class hierarchies are maintained. That is, although rhetorical performances demystify the power of white supremacy, they leave untouched the social stratification assumed by bourgeois liberalism. See the rhetorical enforcement of hierarchy discussed in Wadlington, *The Confidence Game in American Literature*, pp. 258–71.

19 "Corn-Pone Opinions," in *What Is Man? and Other Philosophical Writings*, ed. Paul Baender (Berkeley: University of California Press, 1973), p. 96; *Mark Twain's Notebooks and Journals*, vol. 3, ed. Robert Pack Browning, Michael B. Frank, and Lin Salamo (Berkeley: University of California Press, 1979), p. 88.

20 Burke, *The Philosophy of Literary Form*, p. 110.

21 Actually, Brooks's friend, Waldo Frank, had introduced the thesis a few months earlier in *Our America* (New York: Boni & Liveright, 1919), pp. 38–44; however, it was Brooks's more extended argument that later criticism took up and established as the starting point for debate.

22 Van Wyck Brooks, *The Ordeal of Mark Twain* (New York: Dutton, 1920), pp. 35–36.

23 Lionel Trilling, Introduction to *The Adventures of Huckleberry Finn* (New York: Rinehart, 1948), pp. v–xviii; T. S. Eliot, Introduction to

The Adventures of Huckleberry Finn (New York: Chanticleer Press, 1950), pp. vii–xvi.

24 Lewis Leary, "Standing with Reluctant Feet," in *A Casebook on Mark Twain's Wound,* ed. Leary (New York: Thomas Y. Crowell, 1962), p. 30.

25 Leo Marx, "Mr. Eliot, Mr. Trilling, and *Huckleberry Finn,*" *American Scholar* 22 (Autumn 1953):423–40. Whether Trilling's analysis is *only* a formalist reading is beside the point. The fact that Trilling reprinted the essay in *The Liberal Imagination: Essays on Literature and Society* (New York: Viking Press, 1950, pp. 100–13) suggests that at least the author saw it as part of a broader project in the politics of culture. However, what is crucial for *Huckleberry Finn*'s critical history is that later interpreters, particularly Marx, responded to Trilling's essay as primarily a piece of formalist criticism.

26 The critical move made here can be found in its exemplary form in Stanley Fish, *Is There a Text in This Class? The Authority of Interpretive Communities* (Cambridge, Mass.: Harvard University Press, 1980), pp, 150–2. The rhetorical perspective used throughout my essay is indebted to certain versions of reader-response criticism, but it attempts to move beyond the ahistorical and apolitical approach presented in my *Interpretive Conventions: The Reader in the Study of American Fiction* (Ithaca, N.Y.: Cornell University Press, 1982).

27 *Buffalo Express,* November 8, 1969, p. 2.

28 As James Cox says about *Innocents Abroad* (*Mark Twain,* p. 55).

Notes on Contributors

Michael Davitt Bell, who is J. Leland Miller Professor of American History, Literature, and Eloquence at Williams College, has published *The Development of American Romance* and is preparing *The Problem of American Realism.*

Louis J. Budd is James B. Duke Professor of English at Duke University and managing editor of *American Literature.* Most recently, he has published *Our Mark Twain: The Making of His Public Personality.*

Janet Holmgren McKay, a faculty member in the Department of Linguistics, is Assistant to the Chancellor at the University of Maryland. She has published *Narration and Discourse in American Realistic Fiction,* which combines her interests in discourse analysis and literary style.

Steven Mailloux, who continues to work in rhetoric and critical theory, has published *Interpretive Conventions: The Reader in the Study of American Fiction.* He is Associate Professor of English at the University of Maimi.

Lee Clark Mitchell is Associate Professor of English at Princeton University. Also especially interested in Henry James and Stephen Crane, he has published *Witnesses to a Vanishing America: The Nineteenth-Century Response.*

Selected Bibliography

For the text of *Adventures of Huckleberry Finn*, this collection refers to the 1985 edition in the Mark Twain Library prepared for the University of California Press by the Mark Twain Project (Bancroft Library, University of California). It is based upon the text that Walter Blair and Victor Fischer established for the Iowa/California Edition of The Works of Mark Twain. Besides offering the most authoritative text, it reproduces all the illustrations from the first edition of 1885.

Most books and hundreds of essay about Mark Twain's career touch upon *Huckleberry Finn*. This list gives a cross- section of the most significant criticism from the major points of view.

Bellamy, Gladys. *Mark Twain as a Literary Artist*. Norman: University of Oklahoma Press, 1950.

Blair, Walter. *Mark Twain & Huck Finn*. Berkeley: University of California Press, 1960.

Branch, Edgar M. *The Literary Apprenticeship of Mark Twain*. Urbana: University of Illinois Press, 1950.

Bridgman, Richard. "Henry James and Mark Twain," in his *The Colloquial Style in America*. New York: Oxford University Press, 1966, pp. 78–130.

Carrington, George C., Jr. *The Dramatic Unity of "Huckleberry Finn."* Columbus: Ohio State University Press, 1976.

Covici, Pascal, Jr. *Mark Twain's Humor*. Dallas: Southern Methodist University Press, 1962.

Cox, James M. *Mark Twain: The Fate of Humor*. Princeton, N.J.: Princeton University Press, 1966.

DeVoto, Bernard. "Noon and the Dark − *Huckleberry Finn*," in his *Mark Twain at Work*. Cambridge, Mass.: Harvard University Press, 1942, pp. 45–104.

Dyson, A. E. "*Huckleberry Finn* and the Whole Truth." *Critical Quarterly* 3 (Spring 1961):29–40. Reprinted in his *The Crazy Fabric: Essays in Irony*. New York: St. Martin's Press, 1965.

Selected Bibliography

Emerson, Everett. *The Authentic Mark Twain: A Literary Biography of Samuel L. Clemens.* Philadelphia: University of Pennsylvania Press, 1984.

Ferguson, J. DeLancey. *Mark Twain: Man and Legend.* Indianapolis: Bobbs-Merrill, 1943.

Fischer, Victor. "Huck Finn Reviewed: The Reception of *Huckleberry Finn* in the United States, 1885–1897." *American Literary Realism, 1865–1910* 16 (Spring 1983):1–57.

Gerber, John C. "Mark Twain's Use of the Comic Pose." *PMLA* 77 (June 1962):297–304.

Gibson, William M. *The Art of Mark Twain.* New York: Oxford University Press, 1976.

Hoffman, Daniel G. "Black Magic – and White – in *Huckleberry Finn,*" in his *Form and Fable in American Fiction.* New York: Oxford University Press, 1961, pp. 315–50.

Kaplan, Justin. *Mr. Clemens and Mark Twain.* New York: Simon & Schuster, 1966.

Lynn, Kenneth S. *Mark Twain and Southwestern Humor.* Boston: Little, Brown, 1959.

Marx, Leo. "Mr. Eliot, Mr. Trilling, and *Huckleberry Finn.*" *American Scholar* 22 (Autumn 1953):423–40.

Sattelmeyer, Robert, and Crowley, J. Donald, eds. *One Hundred Years of "Huckleberry Finn": The Boy, His Book, and American Culture.* Columbia: University of Missouri Press, 1985.

Schacht, Paul. "The Lonesomeness of Huckleberry Finn." *American Literature* 53 (May 1981):189–201.

Schmitz, Neil. *Of Huck and Alice: Humorous Writing in American Literature.* Minneapolis: University of Minnesota Press, 1983.

Seelye, John. *The True Adventures of Huckleberry Finn.* Evanston, Ill.: Northwestern University Press, 1970.

Smith, Henry Nash. *Mark Twain: The Development of a Writer.* Cambridge, Mass.: Harvard University Press, 1962.

Stone, Albert E., Jr. *The Innocent Eye: Childhood in Mark Twain's Imagination.* New Haven, Conn.: Yale University Press, 1961.

Tanner, Tony. "Mark Twain," in his *The Reign of Wonder.* Cambridge: Cambridge University Press, 1965, pp. 97–183.

Trachtenberg, Alan. "The Form of Freedom in *Adventures of Huckleberry Finn.*" *Southern Review* NS 6 (October 1970):954–71.